Communication in Marriage Workbook

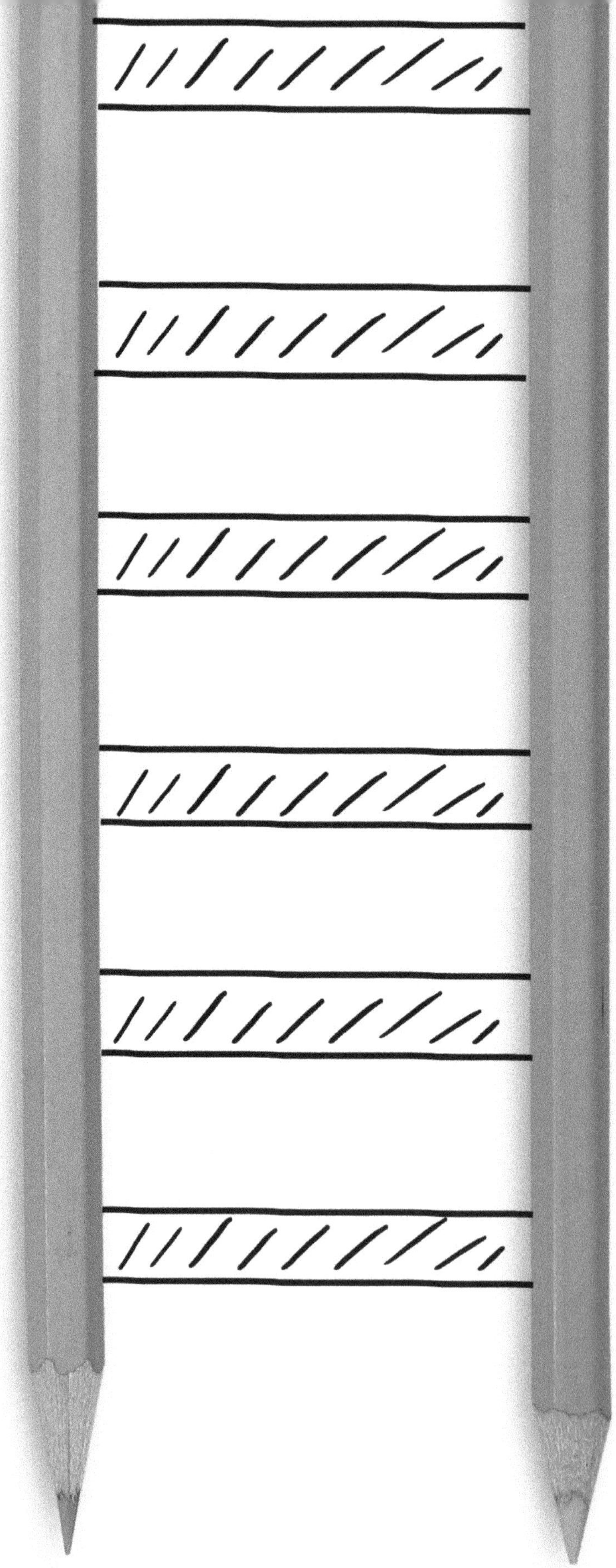

Communication in Marriage
Workbook

Exercises to Resolve Conflict and Improve Your Relationship

Emelie A. Blank, MA, LPC

ROCKRIDGE
PRESS

Interior and Cover Designer: Karmen Lizzul
Art Producer: Samantha Ulban
Editor: Nadina Persaud
Production Editor: Rachel Taenzler

All images used under license © iStock. Author Photo courtesy of © Alyssa Ray.

ISBN: Print 978-1-64739-130-0 | eBook 978-1-64739-131-7
R0

To Julian—
here's to years and years of more communication!

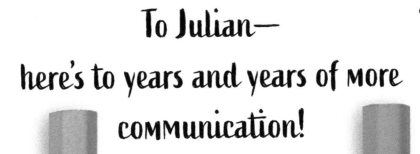

We found each other in the cosmos,
and that was wonderful.
—Ann Druyan

Contents

Introduction

Marriage isn't always easy. Our culture loves to celebrate the fun, romantic parts of marriage, like throwing the wedding of your dreams or sharing a social media post about being in love with your best friend. But it doesn't give us the tools we need to handle marriage when it's not picture-perfect.

My goal with this workbook is to teach you skills you may not have learned about how to be in a relationship with another human being—specifically communication and conflict-management skills.

As a licensed professional counselor, I work with couples of all kinds, including those from communities that are traditionally underserved—the LGBTQIA+ population, polyamorous and non-monogamous folks, and modern couples who are reinventing what marriage means to them. I help all of these people learn the skills they need to have a safe, healthy, and happy marriage. Counseling couples is a unique practice, and I'm excited to be able to pass along to you my experiences and expertise from the therapy room.

In my first book, *Easy Marriage Counseling,* I explored 52 different topics that often come up in couples counseling sessions. Now, through this workbook, I'll help you and your partner discuss a broad range of topics, many of which cause friction in relationships, including household responsibilities and finances, career and lifestyle issues, friends and family, sexuality and intimacy, and overall trust. My goal is to help the two of you build and nurture a strong sense of connection and deepen your communication with one another.

Part 1 describes different aspects of communication and conflict resolution—the good, the bad, and the ugly. We'll go through a variety of techniques and skills, all of which will help you as you do the activities in part 2.

The second part of the book features a number of different activities, including quizzes, exercises, discussion prompts, and educational blurbs. Some activities you and your partner will do together; some are to be completed independently. Some you'll do individually, and then you'll come back together to share your results. All of these activities are designed to increase positive communication between you and your partner and help you to learn more about each other.

The chapters and activities in part 2 do not need to be completed in any specific order, and you're welcome to take them at your own pace. Some of the topics may not apply to your specific partnership. It's also possible that some topics will bring forth feelings that you and your partner will have to thoughtfully address together. Although some topics may lead to difficult or uncomfortable conversations, having these conversations can help you resolve conflicts before they come up and help prevent conflicts in the future.

Good communication is the heart of all healthy relationships, and its place in successful marriages is unparalleled. Whether you and your partner are newlyweds or have been married for decades, whether you have kids or no kids, whether you consider your marriage to be traditional or nontraditional, this book gives you the tools for effective communication so you'll be able to work through common conflicts in a way that ultimately supports your partnership.

A Couple's Agreement

Before you begin, I encourage the two of you to make an agreement about how you want to work through this book. Do you want to cover a chapter/topic a week? Or do you hope to get through the whole book in a weekend?

Whatever you decide, I do recommend making a commitment to work through this book on a regular schedule. Just like in couples therapy, consistency will give you the best results!

I also encourage you to discuss what to do if a certain chapter or activity makes either of you feel uncomfortable, causes distress, or creates conflict between you. A good option is to agree to take a break and then come back to check in with your partner about what you're each feeling. Discuss and agree now how you might support each other if difficult feelings come up during any of the activities.

Finally, I encourage you to keep an open mind and an open heart toward your partner as you get into the weeds of this book together. Discomfort is normal when you're challenging norms in your relationship. Discomfort means you're growing. And there's always room for growth, even on your best days together.

Bravery is required in an honest, authentic relationship. But relationships should also be fun! So be sure to enjoy the fun conversations you'll have as you go through the book, even as you grow from the tough ones.

PART ONE

THE Foundations OF Communication

Here in part 1, I'll discuss individual communication styles and how they impact relationships. I'll also share some key communication skills and conflict management strategies.

As you read through these chapters, I invite you and your partner to think about how you're communicating. What communication skills are you already good at? What might you need to work on? I'll give you ways to change communication habits that may be challenging to your relationship as well as ways to strengthen communication skills that are already working for you.

CHAPTER 1

Communication Fundamentals

Everything you do with your partner involves communication. And communication isn't just your language or verbal communication. Even things you usually don't think of as communication totally are—your body language, tone of voice, facial expressions, an eye roll.

Communicating in a safe, effective way will decrease the number and intensity of the conflicts that you're sure to have with your partner. Safe communication means that both partners are able to feel emotionally safe when communicating with each other.

You've made a big commitment to each other—to have, to hold, and to argue with them, 'til death or divorce do you part. It's in both of your best interests for those conflicts to go as smoothly as possible. And healthy communication is the key to successful conflict management.

Your Communication Style

There are a number of different communication styles. For simplicity, I've separated them into contrasting types, but keep in mind that they're not black and white. Most people utilize all of these styles to varying degrees rather than using just one style or another.

It's also possible that you may use different communication styles in different situations. For example, I find that I can be more direct with my clients about a difficult or uncomfortable topic than I might be with my partner.

Take a look at the following styles and see which ones resonate with you. Keep in mind that none of these styles is right or wrong.

Direct or Indirect

Direct communicators are more likely to share their thoughts, feelings, and needs frankly with their partner. Indirect communicators might rely on body language, tone, or their history with their partner to fully communicate their thoughts, feelings, and needs.

To someone more used to indirect communication, a direct communicator might come off as aggressively straightforward. To someone more used to direct communication, an indirect communicator might come off as passive-aggressive.

Knowing how directly or indirectly your partner tends to communicate can help you "translate" their meaning. Where I might say, "Heck no!" to an invitation to do something I don't want to do, my partner might say "Maybe" when they don't want to do something. I have had to learn that sometimes their maybe is actually a no and sometimes my "Heck no!" should really be a "No, thank you."

Competitive or Affiliative

Whose side are you on? When you're communicating with your partner, do you feel as if you're in competition with them or that the two of you are on the same team?

A competitive communicator frequently needs to be right or often perceives what their partner says as a personal criticism. A competitive communicator might struggle to wait for their partner to finish a thought before presenting their side of the story or their opinion.

An affiliative communicator usually aims to see their partner's point of view. They are more likely to validate their partner than dismiss or challenge them.

I think we all can aim for more affiliative communication in our relationships, especially during conflict. If you struggle with competitive communication, it can be helpful for you to stop and think before speaking during conflict. Slow down your responses, and evaluate whether what you want to say demonstrates that you're on your partner's side or your own side. Aiming for a team dynamic, even amid challenges, can strengthen your relationship.

Amplifying or Condensing

In communication lingo, an amplifier is someone who tends to use a lot of verbal communication to process ideas. They're "talkers." A condenser is someone who usually doesn't need a lot of words to process ideas. Processing for a condenser is short, sweet, and largely internal; it may also leave their partner wondering what they're thinking.

In heterosexual partnerships, it's common for women to be amplifiers, while men tend to be condensers (though this isn't a hard-and-fast rule).

Overamplifiers can strive to do more internal processing instead of relying on verbal debriefings with their partners to help them process ideas. Condensers can strive to do some more processing out loud so their partner knows what's going on with them.

Hot or Cold

What's the temperature of your communication? Are you cold, distant, and stoic? Warm, inviting, and comfortable? Hot, biting, and spicy?

Communication at the far ends of the spectrum (very hot or very cold) can be problematic. Communication that rapidly changes from hot to cold is also a problem; the unpredictability can make partners feel like they're riding on a roller coaster.

For best results, aim for communication that's consistently in the middle of the temperature spectrum—not too hot, not too cold, but just right.

How to Communicate Safely during Conflicts

I can't tell you that good communication will keep you from arguing or that communicating during conflicts is ever going to be easy. Conflicts often bring up a lot of emotions, and when we feel heated, frustrated, activated, or emotionally overloaded, we aren't able to access the full functionality of our brain. As a result, our communication can quickly break down when we're upset.

Unfortunately, most of us, as we were growing up, weren't taught how to communicate effectively when we're upset. But you can learn how to now. Here are some communication skills to help you both feel emotionally safe during a conflict.

Accept Responsibility

When you find yourself in conflict, put yourself in your partner's shoes and accept responsibility for your part. You could say something like, "I'm sorry for how I (or my behavior) played a part in this conflict. What can I do next time instead?"

It might seem pretty basic, but accepting responsibility for your part of the conflict is one of the best moves you can make. It helps your partner feel heard and validated, and it prevents you from making your partner feel guilty or blamed for your actions.

Communication Patterns to Avoid

Research by psychologist John Gottman suggests that avoiding conflict is a bigger predictor for relationship distress than arguing is. Many couples in healthy relationships argue; some even raise their voices. What's important is that both partners feel comfortable with each other's temperament. For example, yelling during an argument can be healthy if both partners are comfortable and safe.

However, some types of communication are emotionally abusive and must always be avoided:

» Making threats or intimidating your partner
» Blaming your partner for your behavior
» Name-calling
» Using put-downs or humiliating your partner
» Gaslighting or making your partner think that they're crazy
» Being overly critical
» Using manipulation to get needs met
» Guilt-tripping
» Minimizing or denying your partner's feelings

If you think you or your partner struggles with any of these patterns, seek professional help. Moving on from these patterns is crucial for the health of your relationship.

To accept responsibility, you may need to reframe your idea of what "winning" in conflict looks like. Does winning an argument mean not taking the blame for something or for the conflict itself? Or does it mean that you and your partner find a resolution together, as a team?

If you're unable to accept responsibility, you might find yourself stuck at an impasse, unable to resolve a conflict.

Avoid Negativity and Contempt

Contempt refers to a general feeling of negativity toward your partner. Contempt can encourage unhealthy dynamics in a relationship. In fact, contempt in relationships is said to be the number one predictor for divorce.

You may feel frustrated with your partner from time to time, but if you feel a consistent level of anger or hostility toward your partner, it's time to seek professional help.

Negative feelings have a way of coming out, one way or another, whether it's through needless criticism, emotional abuse, name-calling, or emotional explosions. You can quash negativity and keep it from growing into contempt by making a conscious effort to communicate your feelings directly to your partner. You can also *make* a habit of identifying things you love about your partner. Finally, you can challenge negative thoughts you might have about your partner in the moment.

Watch Your Tone

Verbal communication involves so much more than the words we say. Couples tend to report that their partner's tone is one of the strongest factors that pushes a disagreement into conflict. I'm sure you can think of a time when what you or your partner said was incongruent with their tone. Maybe they said, "I'm fine," when their tone suggested that things were not, in fact, fine.

Even when you're in the midst of an argument, pay attention to the way you're communicating, including the volume, tone, and inflections of your voice, as well as your words and the way you're weaving sentences together.

Changing your tone can change the way you fight. If you think nonverbal aspects of communication may be a problem for you, focus on slowing down when you're talking. Be deliberate in not just what you say but also how you say it. Keep your voice low, your tone kind, and your language nonjudgmental.

Validate Your Partner

Validating is one of the strongest communication skills you can use during a conflict. Validating means paying attention to what your partner is saying, zeroing in on their meaning, and reflecting back what you heard your partner say to make sure you've heard them accurately. The goal is for your partner to feel heard.

Reflecting can be as simple as repeating back what your partner has said, or you can paraphrase it. Try saying something like, "What I'm hearing is that you're feeling frustrated because of (blank). Am I getting that right?"

In addition to hearing your partner's words, you're also sensing their intention and paying attention to their feelings.

Validating gives you a chance to step away from your heated emotions. It shifts your focus from arguing to understanding. It's hard to argue when you're really listening to your partner. And when your partner feels heard, they're more likely to be willing to listen to you.

Manage Your Emotions

If any of these communication skills feel too challenging in the moment, it's time to take a break and focus on your own emotional regulation. This gives you an opportunity to cool yourself down.

Some couples have a code word or a signal that indicates they're feeling emotionally out of control and need a break. Before your next conflict, talk with your partner about your signals and what taking a break might look like so they know what to expect. If your signal is walking away, for example, you want your partner to know in advance that it means you need to calm down and that you will come back.

Also determine in advance what a reasonable amount of time for a break is. Five minutes, an hour, a day—the length of a typical break is up to you and your partner.

Expand Your Communication Skills

We talked about ways to manage communication during conflicts. Now I'll give you some additional skills that can increase positive communication with your partner. These are skills you can hone during your typical, everyday interactions.

As you put them to use, remember that no one communicates perfectly 100 percent of the time. But practicing these skills can help you keep communication with your partner as healthy as possible.

The 48-Hour Rule

Sometimes we get into conflicts that seem silly after the fact. I've certainly picked an argument over something that later seemed pretty innocuous. Sometimes I don't even remember what started the fight. I just remember how crappy I felt during the argument.

The next time you're feeling frustrated with your partner, try the 48-hour rule: Take about 48 hours to see if what you're simmering about is truly a concern about the relationship or if the frustration is fleeting.

I know I'm more likely to feel frustrated with my partner if I'm hungry, tired, or stressed or because of a multitude of other factors. If I'm able to wait a day or two before voicing my frustration, I may discover that I'm really not frustrated anymore. It may not even be necessary to wait a full 48 hours; sometimes just waiting until the next day changes my perspective.

If you're still frustrated after 48 hours, there's probably something you need to address. Find a calm moment to check in with your partner. Even if you're still frustrated, you're not going to be as heated as you would have been if you had brought up your frustration right away.

Active Listening

Active listening is a skill of attention and reflection.

The first goal of active listening is to be fully present in the experience of communicating with your partner. Facing your partner, making eye contact, and leaning in to hear what they are saying will show your partner that you're present and actively engaging in the conversation. You may also need to eliminate distractions, like the TV or your smartphone.

The next goals of active listening are to listen nonjudgmentally and to confirm that you've accurately heard what your partner is saying. You want to make sure you understand their meaning, especially when they're saying something important. To do that, you reflect—you summarize their statements and repeat the summary back to them. Then they can confirm whether you've heard them correctly.

Empathy

Empathy is the ability to understand what your partner might be feeling. Empathy doesn't mean actually feeling what your partner is feeling but *understanding* what your partner is feeling. Empathy can help you see things from your partner's perspective and understand why they're feeling a specific way.

To incorporate a sense of empathy into a situation, you can aim to predict what your partner might be feeling and use this prediction to anticipate what they might need from you. Here's a basic example: Your partner has just broken their leg. You understand that the pain is causing them to cry. A level beyond that might be recognizing that their pain affects their ability to walk, so you carry them or help them limp to the car. At home, you recognize that your partner can't do as much around the house while their leg is healing, so you pick up the extra chores and tasks as they recover.

Body Language

Body language tells you a lot about what another person is thinking or feeling. If your partner is nodding, facing toward you, or leaning in toward you, most likely they're interested in your conversation and what you're saying. But perhaps your partner is turning away from you, not making eye contact, crossing their arms, or looking agitated, hypervigilant, or twitchy. These body language cues communicate a lack of interest in the conversation or a feeling of unease.

Facial expressions and movements, such as nodding your head, are other examples of body language. They indicate how you're feeling in response to what your partner is saying.

It's important that your body language be in tune with your words. If you're saying one thing but your body language is telling a different story, which is your partner to believe?

The absence of body language is part of the reason communication by text, phone, email, or even video chat might not feel as clear as face-to-face communication. When you and your partner are discussing something important, face-to-face communication is usually the best option because body language can be part of the conversation.

Interest

Showing interest is an important part of being a good communication partner. Besides using body language (see the previous section), asking questions and providing feedback verbally are great ways to show your interest.

For example, if your partner is describing a rude customer at work, you could ask a clarifying question like, "So you mean that the customer said _____ to you?" Or you could give feedback like, "Wow, you handled that situation really well!" You could even provide your opinion or perspective, if it's relevant or welcomed, such as, "I would have responded like this . . ." All of these responses are ways of showing interest in what your partner is saying.

Directness

I frequently hear couples say that they're having a hard time understanding one another, even though they're communicating quite often. Speaking indirectly often contributes to this problem.

Say you ask your partner if they want to get dinner at a new sushi restaurant. Your partner says, "I don't know. Maybe." This indirect answer might leave you wondering how your partner really feels and why. Are they too busy with work to decide? Are they worried about finances? Are they mad at you? Are they not in the mood for fish? The possibilities are endless.

When communicating with your partner, make it your goal to be as clear, concise, and direct as possible without being unkind. A lot might be misunderstood when you don't!

The Listening Factor

When couples are struggling through communication breakdowns, an all-too-common defense is "I'm just not a good listener." Listening is a skill we learn, not a natural ability we are born with. It's something all partners need to work on.

Listening requires more than just having your ears and eyes open. In addition to using active listening and showing interest, as described in the previous section, here are some ways you can improve your listening:

Stay engaged. Don't get lost in your own thoughts. Focus your attention on the person in front of you. Listen not only to their words but also to their body language, tone, and volume. Think about what they're saying and how what they're sharing might be affecting them. Use active listening to stay engaged and to keep yourself accountable for paying attention.

Validate. Show your partner you understand what they're communicating by not only reflecting what they said but also acknowledging how they feel. Validate their feelings and let them know you're on their team.

Notice your listening habits. Pay a little bit of attention to what you're doing when you're listening. What is your body doing? What is happening in your mind? How might you be coming across?

Emulate good listeners. Notice what you see other people doing well when they listen, and try doing those same things yourself. For example, if you like that your partner sets down their phone when you have something to tell them, try doing the same thing when they want to talk. Also ask your partner what they appreciate in a listener and work to listen in the way they describe.

Ask for feedback. Ask your partner to tell you what you do well when listening and how you could improve. Take your partner's feedback seriously and aim to implement it where you can. Give your partner suggestions too, if they ask.

Five Communication Commitments

In addition to practicing the skills in this chapter, there are five commitments you and your partner can make to support positive communication and a long, happy, strong relationship. As you review them, think about which commitments the two of you are already following and which you might need to work on.

Express Yourself Freely

It's our responsibility to stand up for ourselves, express ourselves, and communicate our needs kindly, clearly, and assertively—*not* aggressively, hurtfully, or indirectly.

In order to feel comfortable sharing our needs, beliefs, feelings, and opinions with our partner, we must feel accepted by our partner. We need to know that our partner will accept whatever we choose to share, even when they have a contrary opinion or belief.

This commitment is a two-way street: It's also our job to listen to our partner without judgment and allow them to express themselves freely, even if we don't always agree with them.

The Art of Compromise

Compromise is a conflict-resolution art. When we choose to make a compromise, we might or might not get exactly what we want. But sometimes a compromise means both partners are able to get their needs met.

There are certain things we might be more comfortable compromising about than others. You and your partner can each ask yourself, "What things am I willing to budge on? What am I not willing to compromise on?" Getting an idea about what is important and not so important to each of you will help you make compromises that work for both of you.

Avoid Mind Reading

Mind reading is when we assume we know what others are thinking or feeling, but we really don't know for sure. You might think, for example, "My partner isn't texting me back because they're mad at me." But what's actually happening could be very different. Perhaps your partner broke their phone. Maybe they got reprimanded at work for texting too much. Maybe they're driving.

We have no way of knowing what others might be thinking or feeling or what might be motivating their behavior without asking them. So instead of assuming you know what your partner is thinking or trying to figure out why they're doing something, just ask them.

Respect Boundaries

Boundaries are lines we draw between one another. Setting boundaries is a way of expressing our personal empowerment in a partnership. Boundaries are crucial in healthy, loving relationships.

Some people fear setting boundaries; they worry that it might push their loved ones away. Other people might set very firm boundaries because they fear getting too close. But boundary setting means we care about having a relationship that feels good, and it reduces negative feelings we might have when our needs are not met.

It's our job to set our own personal boundaries and to respect the boundaries of our partner. Having respect for our partner, our relationship, and ourselves means that we are constantly evaluating and setting our own personal boundaries and encouraging our partner to do the same.

Boundaries should not be set or met with resentment, negativity, anger, or frustration. Conversations about boundaries are best had when both partners are calm, ready to listen, and able to be respectful of each other.

Make Sure All Criticism Is Productive

We should never feel eager to give our partner unproductive criticism. Criticism is unproductive when it's malicious or meant to hurt the other person. This kind of criticism breeds contempt, which is a proven relationship killer.

Criticism is productive when it's focused on a specific scenario or situation, aimed at fostering positive change, and delivered kindly. This kind of criticism is more likely to be well received than unproductive criticism.

Rebuild Trust When Needed

There will come a time in your relationship where someone has made a mistake. This mistake could be relationship altering or even relationship ending. If you and your partner choose to continue your relationship after trust has been broken, it's your mutual responsibility to rebuild the trust between you.

Rebuilding trust takes open and honest communication as well as healthy boundary setting. It requires you to make an effort to build trust and be receptive to your partner's efforts.

It may take time to feel ready to rebuild trust—maybe days, weeks, months, even a year or more. However, if you want to continue to be in the relationship, eventually you will rebuild your trust.

Building and rebuilding trust look different for every partnership. Chapter 3 will help you explore the topic of trust in depth.

PART TWO

Conflict Management

All right, now we're getting into the good stuff! Here in part 2, you'll identify common challenges in your relationship and come up with different ways to address them. First you'll be evaluating where you are now as a couple. Then you'll work together to find proactive ways to manage conflict and reach solutions that work for both of you.

Some chapter topics might resonate with you or feel more pressing than others. Feel free to take the chapters in whatever order works best for you.

CHAPTER 2

Household Duties, Finances, and Personal Goals

Household management can be one of the most frequent areas of conflict in relationships. Do you know how many dishes-related arguments I've been privy to in the therapy room? Quite a few.

We'll begin by evaluating what's currently going on in your household. Who does what? How do you determine who does what? Do you feel like household duties are handled equitably?

It's important to remember that you can manage your household in whatever way you see fit. What's important is that both you and your partner feel respected and have a say in the division of household labor. I'm not going to give you specific rules for managing your household; I'm going to help you find what works for you. I'll also discuss different strategies for getting what you need from your partner when it comes to household work.

Finally, we'll talk about some other tricky household topics that frequently trigger conflict, including money, budgeting, and planning for the future.

ACTIVITY 1: Stages of Change

In therapy, we talk about the stages of change. Here are the different stages of change and what they might look like in a relationship.

STAGE OF CHANGE	DEFINITION	EXAMPLE
Pre-Contemplation	You have no intention of changing your behavior.	Things aren't going well between Alex and Charlie, but neither partner feels responsible for making changes. Both partners deny that there's a problem with the relationship.
Contemplation	You're aware that things need to change, but you have not yet explored what you need to do to make that change.	Alex and Charlie are fighting more often, communicating in passive-aggressive ways, and blaming each other for the problems in the relationship. They want to solve their problems, but they can't determine what needs to change.
Preparation	You begin to think about how you might change and what steps you need to take to adjust our way of being.	Alex and Charlie start to talk more openly, honestly, and directly about what needs to change in the relationship. They start to make an action plan for what they each need to do to work on the relationship.
Action	You are actively working on changing your behavior. You have a plan, and you're following it.	Alex and Charlie are both working on aspects of their personality that create conflict in the relationship. They have identified their problems and have a plan to work things out.
Maintenance	You have successfully made changes and are working to maintain these changes.	Alex and Charlie feel like the problems they had in the beginning are well managed. Other issues in the relationship might crop up, but both are committed to changing the dynamics of the relationship.

STAGE OF CHANGE	DEFINITION	EXAMPLE
Relapse	Whoops, you slipped back into old habits! From this stage, you might jump back into any of the previous stages.	Alex and Charlie have fallen back into old patterns that hurt the relationship. After an honest conversation, they're able to reorient to their goal of maintaining a positive connection in their relationship.

ACTIVITY 2: Are You Ready to Change?

As a therapist, I know it's important for me to assess a couple's willingness to change. Often couples come to me with a lot of concerns about the relationship but are not yet ready or willing to make changes.

With this activity, you'll assess what stage of change you and your partner are in right now. Check each statement that applies to you or your feelings about the relationship. At the end, add up the total number of check marks in each section. Whichever section has the most is likely the stage of change you're currently in.

PRE-CONTEMPLATION

PARTNER 1	PARTNER 2	
☐	☐	My partner is the one with the problem, not me.
☐	☐	Even if I were to try to change the relationship, nothing would happen.
☐	☐	Our relationship is perfect and doesn't need to change.
☐	☐	People can't change, so why bother?
☐	☐	Why are we even reading this book?
_____	_____	TOTAL

CONTEMPLATION

PARTNER 1	PARTNER 2	
☐	☐	I think our relationship might need work, but I don't know what to do.
☐	☐	I feel ready to change some of the time, but not all the time.

☐	☐	Something big happened in our relationship, and I think we might need to do something about it.
☐	☐	I'm not sure we can do anything to change the problem.
☐	☐	What if we try to change and it doesn't work?
___	___	TOTAL

PREPARATION

PARTNER 1 PARTNER 2

☐	☐	I'm committed to doing whatever I can to work on our relationship.
☐	☐	I can be open and honest with my partner about what I think the problem is.
☐	☐	I think we can comfortably solve problems without either of us blaming each other.
☐	☐	I have a few ideas on what needs to change.
☐	☐	When are we going to start doing things differently?
___	___	TOTAL

ACTION

PARTNER 1 PARTNER 2

☐	☐	I'm relieved that we're finally addressing the problem.
☐	☐	I think my partner and I are both making adjustments.
☐	☐	Change is hard, but it's working.
☐	☐	I think I'm learning new skills for my relationship.
☐	☐	Some days are great; others are garbage. When will we feel more stable?
___	___	TOTAL

MAINTENANCE

PARTNER 1 PARTNER 2

☐	☐	I catch myself when I start to slip into unhealthy habits.
☐	☐	My partner and I aren't having the same fights all the time.
☐	☐	We don't need to change much more.
☐	☐	It's been a long time since my partner and I had a conflict.
☐	☐	We have ups and downs, but things are good!
_____	_____	**TOTAL**

RELAPSE

PARTNER 1 PARTNER 2

☐	☐	Things seemed better, but not anymore.
☐	☐	It feels like we've returned to the status quo.
☐	☐	I think my partner and I have different goals for change.
☐	☐	The same things keep happening, and I feel frustrated.
☐	☐	Why do we keep having the same conflicts?
_____	_____	**TOTAL**

ACTIVITY 3: Ch-Ch-Ch-Changes

Are you and your partner at the same stage of change?

_____

_____

_____

How does change feel for each of you? Is change scary? Is it easy? Are you some-one who is able to change more readily than others?

_____

_____

_____

What is one specific change that you've attempted to make in the past? Did that change resolve the problem you meant it to?

Partner 1:

_____

_____

Partner 2:

_____

_____

The last time you made a change in your relationship, what did each of you think or do at each stage?

PRE-CONTEMPLATION

Partner 1:

_____

_____

Partner 2:

_____

_____

CONTEMPLATION

Partner 1:

_____

_____

Partner 2:

_____

_____

PREPARATION

Partner 1:

_____

_____

Partner 2:

_____

_____

ACTION

Partner 1:

_____

_____

Partner 2:

_____

_____

MAINTENANCE

Partner 1:

_____

_____

Partner 2:

_____

_____

RELAPSE

Partner 1:

_____

_____

Partner 2:

_____

_____

How do you see this cycle applying to your relationship?

_____

_____

ACTIVITY 4: Equality and Equity

Generally speaking, does it make sense for you and your partner to split household tasks evenly? Or does your equitable solution for household work rely more on one partner?

For each question, circle the letter of the answer that best fits your situation.

1. Do you and your partner both work full-time?

   a. Yes, we both work about the same amount of time in a week.

   b. Yes, and one of us works significantly more than the other.

   c. No, one of us works full-time, and the other doesn't.

2. Do you or your partner have any activities or responsibilities requiring significant, nonnegotiable time commitments outside work hours? Examples: You are taking care of a family member, have a long commute, or have additional employment or projects.

   a. We both have about the same amount of commitments outside our jobs.

   b. Both of us have other commitments, but one of us has more commitments than the other.

   c. Only one of us has commitments outside the workplace.

3. Are there physical or mental factors that make it difficult for you or your partner to contribute to the household management?

   a. We have about the same level of ability to do household tasks.

   b. We both have barriers, but one of us has more than the other.

   c. One of us has barriers; the other does not.

RESULTS

Mostly a's, you and your partner have about the same amount of work hours, additional time commitments, and barriers. A 50-50 split of household labor might make sense for your relationship.

Mostly b's, household labor falls mainly to one partner. Splitting household tasks 50-50 might not feel equitable due to other responsibilities one partner might have.

Mostly c's, it might make sense for one partner to do the majority of the household labor. This doesn't mean that one partner should *always* be responsible for *everything* and the other partner is off the hook. But it does mean that equality might not be equitable in your situation.

ACTIVITY 5: **Who Does What?**

For each of the common household tasks that follow, write a percentage indicating how often each of you does that task in the household.

For each task, your and your partner's percentages together should equal 100 percent. For example, I take out the trash only about 10 percent of the time, and my partner does it 90 percent of the time. I usually make our meals around 75 percent of the time, and my partner might make them 25 percent of the time.

Skip tasks that don't apply.

This activity might bring up some feelings. If you find yourself struggling to have a productive discussion while doing this activity, take a break and come back to it later.

PARTNER 1   PARTNER 2

_____	_____	Doing dishes
_____	_____	Taking out the trash/compost/recycling
_____	_____	Pet care
_____	_____	Floor cleaning
_____	_____	Cleaning/dusting surfaces
_____	_____	Tidying/organizing/picking up clutter
_____	_____	Delegating tasks (reminding your partner to do something)
_____	_____	Running errands
_____	_____	Meal planning/preparation
_____	_____	Cleaning the bathroom
_____	_____	Paying bills
_____	_____	Laundry
_____	_____	Yard work
_____	_____	Car maintenance
_____	_____	Basic household maintenance and repairs
_____	_____	Arranging for household repairs
_____	_____	Planning social activities
_____	_____	Making household decisions (such as what color to paint the walls, what furniture to buy)
_____	_____	Stay-at-home parenting
_____	_____	Taking kids to school
_____	_____	Helping kids with homework, overseeing their chores
_____	_____	Making decisions about how to raise children
_____	_____	Waking kids up, getting them ready for the day
_____	_____	Getting kids ready for bed
_____	_____	Providing or finding medical care for kids, pets, or other family members
_____	_____	Coordinating with teachers, caregivers, vendors, etc.

		Buying gifts, writing cards for children or family
_____	_____	Other: _____
_____	_____	Other: _____
_____	_____	Other: _____
_____	_____	Other: _____

ACTIVITY 6: Make a Weekly Schedule

This activity will show you what you and your partner have going on a weekly basis.

Make a list of all the weekly time commitments that you and your partner have on a separate sheet or calendar app. Below is an example.

Are there any big holes in your schedule? Who has a longer list?

EXAMPLE:

DAY	PARTNER X
Monday	-Go to the gym -Work 9 a.m.–5 p.m. -Finish paperwork at home, answer phone calls -Make dinner

ACTIVITY 7: Let's Check In!

Was there anything that surprised you as you did activities 1 through 6? Do you or your partner do more or less around the house than you thought? Does the amount of household labor you each do feel equitable?

Discuss the previous activities and, as a couple, write down some of the ideas that come up in the discussion.

_____

_____

Did these household management activities show you anything that immediately needs your attention as a couple? If so, what was it?

_____

_____

What household tasks do you have conflicts about the most often? Are the reasons for these arguments clearer now that you've done the previous activities together?

_____

_____

What do you want to change about the way that you and your partner handle household tasks? Are there any tasks you can split more equitably? Is there a better system for determining who does what tasks?

_____

_____

Equity or Equality?

Do you know the difference between equity and equality? _Equality_ means things are totally equal or split 50-50. Equality usually sounds great, but it may not work for every couple. Equity is the idea that things should feel fair. Even though 50-50 might seem like the fairest division of household labor, for example, it may not feel fair to one or both of you.

For example, in my relationship, I don't do a lot of household chores. My partner and I agreed that because I work more hours than they do and they have the flexibility to work from home, it makes more sense for them to manage more of the household tasks. Our household chore loads are unequal because my partner does more around the house than I do. But the loads feel equitable because other things I do for the relationship, such as working more hours and bringing in more income, even things out.

According to a 2004 study from Bartley, Blanton, and Gilliard, when partners feel that their division of labor and contribution to the relationship are equitable, they tend to feel more satisfied in their relationships. Things don't need to be perfectly equal, but they do need to feel equitable.

ACTIVITY 8: Relationship Roles

From activities 1 through 7, you probably gained some information about how your household operates. Along the way, you may have learned something about the different roles each of you plays in your relationship.

The relationship roles that feel good for your partnership might be different than those that feel good to your parents or friends. It's important that you feel comfortable with these roles—not that they fit a specific model.

For each of the following statements, answer "true" if you and your partner agree that the statement is mostly true. Answer "false" if you and your partner agree that the statement is mostly false. Answer "disagree" if you and your partner cannot agree whether the statement is true or false.

1. Both of us contribute when we need to make decisions for our relationship and household.

2. Both of us invest something—money, time, or effort—in our household and relationship.

3. Both of us contribute to our home by doing household chores.

4. Both of us perform emotional labor, such as listening to the other person, validating them, and helping them solve problems when needed.

5. In our home, household tasks are generally divided by skill and interest, not gender stereotypes.

6. Both of us trust each other to make decisions for our relationship and trust that each of us has the best interests of our partnership in mind.

7. Both of us have a sense of who does what in our household.

8. Each of us thinks we're generally responsible for caring for ourselves. Neither of us thinks that our partner needs to parent us.

9. Both of us feel happy with the roles we play in the household.

10. Both of us feel comfortable asking for help, communicating frustration around household roles or tasks, and negotiating or compromising about how things are done in our home.

RESULTS

Mostly "true," you and your partner are mostly on the same page about the choices you've made for your household. You both generally feel that the relationship is equitable, and when it comes to deciding which roles you each play in your household, both of you feel heard.

Mostly "false," there may be a lack of equity or equality in your household roles. It might be time to make some changes.

Mostly "disagree," you and your partner are not on the same page about what is going on in your relationship. One of you might think the partnership is not equitable, or the other might be denying their partner's experience.

> **ACTIVITY 9: What Does Equity Look Like for Your Partnership?**

In activity 8, which statements did you and your partner answer "false" or "disagree"?

_____

_____

_____

_____

Why did you answer "false" or "disagree" with some statements?

_____

_____

_____

_____

How do you feel about the fact that you disagreed about some statements? Do you think these disagreements are things that need to be resolved?

Partner 1:

_____

_____

Partner 2:

_____

_____

How do you want to experience equity in your relationship?

_____

_____

_____

Do you feel comfortable with the way your gender roles have an impact on your relationship, or would you like to make adjustments?

_____

_____

_____

_____

ACTIVITY 10: Financial Priorities

What are financial priorities for each of you? Imagine you and your partner have unlimited funds and could check off every single item on the following list. Which would you pay for first? What isn't as important to you? Rank each of the items in the order in which you'd prioritize them.

You and your partner may prioritize different things—and that's okay! The important thing is negotiating appropriately to get the things each of you needs and thinks are important.

PARTNER 1	PARTNER 2	
☐	☐	Buying a home
☐	☐	Paying down debt
☐	☐	Travel, vacations
☐	☐	Clothing and accessories
☐	☐	Dining out
☐	☐	Going out to bars, drinking alcohol
☐	☐	Personal services (e.g., haircuts, manicures, massages)

☐	☐	Your children's future (e.g., education, inheritances)
☐	☐	Luxury items
☐	☐	Career development activities (e.g., trainings, workshops, college courses)
☐	☐	Pets or pet-related expenses
☐	☐	Necessary spending (e.g., utilities, groceries, insurance, medical care)
☐	☐	Buying or paying off a car
☐	☐	Hobbies
☐	☐	Gadgets, technology
☐	☐	Having a child or paying other child-related expenses
☐	☐	Gifts for family, friends, loved ones
☐	☐	Entertainment
☐	☐	Providing long-term care for a family member
☐	☐	Retirement savings
☐	☐	Charitable giving, donations
☐	☐	Other:
☐	☐	Other:
☐	☐	Other:

Do you and your partner have the same top five priorities? What about the same bottom five? Did anything surprise you about your partner's answers?

ACTIVITY 11: Tracking Average Weekly Spending

Let's see if there are any glaring differences in how you and your partner spend and manage money.

On a separate piece of paper, make a table like the one below and record everything you spent money on in the past week, whether it was a necessity, a bill payment, or something fun. Use your bank account or credit card statements to get the most accurate picture of the week's transactions. Make sure you review a typical spending week, as opposed to a week when you were on vacation or making unusual purchases.

Money can be a touchy subject. Don't be afraid to take a break and return to this activity later if this topic feels challenging.

DAY	EXAMPLE	TOTAL	PARTNER 1	TOTAL	PARTNER 2	TOTAL
MONDAY	Breakfast, $2.50 Week's lunch, $20	$22.50				
TUESDAY	Grocery shopping, $60 Gas, $50	$110				
WEEK'S TOTAL SPENDING						

ACTIVITY 12: Making a Budget

Making a budget is probably not the most exciting thing you can do with your partner, but it could help you manage your finances together and increase your communication about one of the most challenging topics for couples to discuss: money.

As you create a monthly budget, it might be helpful to review your bank statements. First, you'll look at what each of you is spending each month. Then you'll see what percentage each of you spends on shared expenses and how much of your current income is being spent.

Keep in mind that in most relationships, the partners do not make the same amount or contribute the same amount to household finances. Money is only part of what you invest in a relationship, and how you manage your finances is a personal decision.

For ongoing budgeting, there are apps that can help the two of you stay on target.

	PARTNER 1	PARTNER 2
Total Monthly Income: wages, bonuses, side hustles, dividends—any money that comes in		
Housing: rent, mortgage		
Utilities: power, gas, internet, trash, water, sewer, etc.		
Transportation: car expenses, bus passes, bike maintenance, etc.		
Medical Expenses: co-pays, medical bills, therapy appointments, complementary care appointments, insurance premiums, etc.		
Food: groceries, dining out, food delivery services, etc.		
Personal Care: toiletries, hygiene products, etc.		
Luxury Items: clothing, high-end products, etc.		
Household Expenses: toilet paper, light bulbs, furniture, etc.		

	PARTNER 1	PARTNER 2
Savings		
Debt Repayment: paying off credit cards, student loans, etc.		
Entertainment: going to a show, Netflix subscription, board games, etc.		
Donations/ Charitable Giving		
Retirement Savings		
Vacation Spending/Saving		
Childcare Expenses		
Extras: child support, alimony, legal fees, etc.		
Other: anything else		

Now let's look at the totals.

	PARTNER 1	PARTNER 2
TOTAL INCOME		
TOTAL SPENDING		

	PARTNER 1	PARTNER 2
PERCENTAGE OF INCOME SPENT		
TOTAL SPENDING ON SHARED EXPENSES		
PERCENTAGE OF SHARED EXPENSES		

Money Stories

More than two-thirds of couples I've polled said that money is one of the biggest sources of conflict in their relationships.

Why is money such a challenge in partnerships? Because we all come from different money stories. Money stories are the personal histories that shape our relationship to money. For example, someone who grew up with plentiful resources is going to have a different relationship to money than someone who grew up with less.

Even folks who come from similar means might have different stories based on how their parents spent. Were they stingy? Generous? Did they discuss money? How did they manage money as a couple? Was one person in charge of financial decisions, or was it a joint effort?

What about debt? Did your family rack up credit card debt?

How did you learn about money and debt? Think about how these patterns come out in your relationship. Some people may repeat the patterns they saw in their family of origin, and some people might reject them.

ACTIVITY 13: Spending Styles

Let's see what spending style best describes your financial habits. Keep in mind that there is no wrong money style.

1. If you got a big tax refund, what would you do with it?
   a. Treat myself to something I've been eyeing.

   b. Put it in a high-interest savings account, in a retirement fund, or toward our mortgage, car loans, credit cards, student loans, or other debt.

   c. Buy something we need but had put off buying, like a new roof or appliance.

   d. Invest in a new business or stocks.

   e. It depends. I might spend some and save some, but I can't say for sure until the time comes.

2. Which statement describes your feelings about money?
   a. Life is worth living, and money is for spending. Leaving money sitting in a bank account doesn't do anything for me.

   b. Spending money makes me feel uncomfortable. I always try to find a deal.

   c. The more money I have saved up, the safer I feel. I want to be prepared for anything.

   d. Money comes in, and it goes out. Sometimes I make good choices with my money; sometimes I don't.

   e. Money doesn't make happiness. I don't care too much about money.

3. Which of these scenarios could you see yourself in?
   a. I spent too much from my last paycheck, so I need to dip into my savings or use a credit card from now until payday.

   b. I cut coupons even when I have a lot of money in the bank.

   c. I maxed out my IRA contribution this year, and I'm switching my savings account to one with a higher interest rate.

   d. I impulsively bought a car I saw on Craigslist. It seemed like a good deal at the time, but now I'm not sure it was.

e. I have no idea how much money is in my bank account, and it doesn't bother me.

4. How do you feel about debt?

a. I have credit card debt, just like most people. Sometimes it's a lot; sometimes it's a little.

b. I would rather eat ramen for every meal than go into debt.

c. I have debt for necessities (like school, a car, or a home) but not for other stuff. I make a point to pay off debts as quickly as I can.

d. Debt is fine if the payout is high. I could buy a house, renovate it, and then sell it for a profit.

e. I have some debt, but I don't worry or think about it much at all.

RESULTS

Mostly a's. You're a super spender. You think money is meant to be spent, and you have no problem racking up a big tab at your favorite restaurant. Your credit card bills might be high, but you have all the fun gadgets you want. You may be impulsive when it comes to spending.

Mostly b's. You're a super saver. You find it hard to part with your hard-earned cash. You might resist buying things for yourself and often buy things on sale or secondhand. You might experience anxiety when you spend money or feel like money is hard to come by.

Mostly c's. You're risk avoidant. You make "responsible" choices with your money. You save wisely, and you might feel well prepared for retirement. Like the saver, you might struggle to make fun purchases.

Mostly d's. You're a risk taker. You might gamble on a big investment that might or might not pay off. You trust your gut when it comes to spending but may not do a lot of research about what you spend money on.

Mostly e's. You're money-meh. You don't think too much about money. You're comfortable regardless of whether you have a lot of zeroes in your bank account or are waiting for payday. You might be one to rack up overdraft fees because you don't keep track of how much money you have. Being in debt doesn't bother you too much, at least not most of the time.

ACTIVITY 14: Let's Talk Money

Do you and your partner have the same spending style or different ones? (See activity 13.) Have you noticed similarities or differences in your spending styles before, or is this new information?

_____

_____

_____

Have you ever had a conflict because of the different ways you and your partner prioritize and spend money? How did this conflict emerge? What did you and your partner learn about each other or your relationship from this conflict?

_____

_____

_____

_____

What's your money story? Where did you learn about money, debt, and spending?

Partner 1:

_____

_____

_____

Partner 2:

_____

_____

_____

As you did activities 10 to 13, was there anything that surprised you about how your partner spends, budgets, or thinks about money?

Partner 1:

_____

_____

_____

Partner 2:

_____

_____

_____

What budgeting or spending compromises can you and your partner make? How can you communicate better about money in the future?

_____

_____

_____

_____

_____

ACTIVITY 15: Your Goals and Dreams

What goals do you and your partner have for your individual lives and for your relationship? Let's find out where you share some of the same hopes and dreams for the future.

Put a check mark beside the following dreams or goals that mean the most to you. Feel free to add your own unique goals to the end of the list.

PARTNER 1 PARTNER 2

☐	☐	Owning a home
☐	☐	Working from home
☐	☐	Retiring at your desired retirement age
☐	☐	Starting a new career
☐	☐	Increasing your income
☐	☐	Having, adopting, or fostering a child or children
☐	☐	Improving or maintaining your physical health
☐	☐	Traveling
☐	☐	Learning a new skill or taking up a new hobby
☐	☐	Living a year or more in a different place

☐	☐	Learning a new language
☐	☐	Continuing your education
☐	☐	Eliminating debt
☐	☐	Being financially stable
☐	☐	Exploring faith or spirituality
☐	☐	Improving or supporting your mental health
☐	☐	Improving your parenting, learning new parenting strategies
☐	☐	Philanthropic activities
☐	☐	Improving or maintaining your work-life balance
☐	☐	Reading more books
☐	☐	Going on a date with your partner once a week
☐	☐	Trying adventure/action/extreme sports, such as skydiving, base jumping, or hang gliding
☐	☐	Decluttering your home
☐	☐	Spending more time with friends and family
☐	☐	Being more efficient at work or school
☐	☐	Finishing a creative project, like writing a novel, filming a documentary, starting a podcast, etc.
☐	☐	Increasing sexual satisfaction and intimacy
☐	☐	Having more positive communication with your partner
☐	☐	Finishing a major athletic endeavor, like running a marathon
☐	☐	Starting a business or working for yourself
☐	☐	Improving your credit score
☐	☐	Taking care of a family member who needs help
☐	☐	Mentoring others
☐	☐	Other:
☐	☐	Other:
☐	☐	Other:

ACTIVITY 16: Moving Toward Your Goals

From the previous activity, what were your top three individual goals?

Partner 1:

_____

_____

_____

Partner 2:

_____

_____

_____

What actions or steps are you taking to work on these personal goals?

Partner 1:

_____

_____

_____

Partner 2:

_____

_____

_____

Is there anything you need from your partner in order to complete these goals?

Partner 1:

_____

_____

_____

Partner 2:

_____

_____

_____

As a couple, what are your top three shared goals?

_____

_____

_____

What actions or steps are you working on to accomplish these shared goals? What do you need from each other to achieve these?

_____

_____

_____

_____

ACTIVITY 17: Your Goals and Dreams

Is one of you more or less motivated than the other when it comes to accomplishing your individual or relationship goals?

_____

_____

_____

_____

_____

What has prevented you from taking steps toward meeting your goals in the past? How can you avoid these obstacles in the future?

Partner 1:

_____

_____

Partner 2:

_____

_____

_____

Imagine what you want your future life together to look like. How is it different than the life you have today? How is it similar? Together, collaborate on a shared vision.

_____

_____

_____

_____

_____

ACTIVITY 18: Future Planning

The last question of activity 17 gave you a good idea of what you want your future life to look like. What do you need to do to turn that vision into a reality?

Make a list of the things you need to or want to accomplish in the short term, longer term, and very long term. What are your individual goals, and how do you get there? What are your goals for your relationship? How do you think your goals, priorities, or values might change over time?

	PARTNER 1'S GOALS	PARTNER 2'S GOALS	SHARED RELATIONSHIP GOALS
6 MONTHS			
1 YEAR			
2 YEARS			

	PARTNER 1'S GOALS	PARTNER 2'S GOALS	SHARED RELATIONSHIP GOALS
5 YEARS			
10 YEARS			

ACTIVITY 19: End-of-Chapter Check-In

Let's see how you and your partner think you've been communicating so far. For each statement below, answer "true," "false," or "we disagree."

1. Both of us feel that we were able to share our thoughts, feelings, and opinions openly and honestly during this chapter's activities.

2. Both of us feel that we were able to listen to each other's thoughts and feelings.

3. Both of us feel that we were able to communicate about these issues calmly, appropriately, and safely.

4. Both of us feel that we were able to take a nonjudgmental stance when we disagreed on something.

5. Both of us feel confident that we understand each other's perspectives on the topics we discussed.

6. Each of us learned something new or surprising about the other person.

RESULTS

Mostly "true," you and your partner were likely able to complete the activities while remaining on the same team. You were able to hear each other's opinions, even if you disagreed. Great job communicating effectively in this chapter!

Mostly "false," you and your partner may have been challenged by certain aspects of this chapter. I invite you to return to topics that you continue to feel unsettled by and to work to resolve communication challenges before moving on. If you thought you didn't do a good job of speaking openly or listening fully, you can go back and try again.

Mostly "disagree," you and your partner are not on the same page about how things went. The two of you may not be fully understanding each other. I advise you to have a heart-to-heart talk about what's getting in the way of your mutual understanding and discuss ways you can overcome these barriers.

Household Duties, Finances, and Personal Goals: Five Takeaways

1. **Change.** Reflect on where we're at in the stages of change.

2. **Equity, not equality**. Everything doesn't need to be split 50-50, but everything does need to feel fair to both of you.

3. **Relationship roles.** Do you both feel good in your roles?

4. **Money.** Practice having difficult conversations about finances and continue to practice this as time goes on!

5. **Future planning.** Goal planning is a crucial step for couples of all developmental stages.

Household Duties, Finances, and Personal Goals: Five Conflict-Management Strategies

1. **Change.** Work on accepting what stage of change your partner is in. You cannot force or expect your partner to change. Work on appreciating your partner for who they are now instead of who you might want them to be.

2. **Equity, not equality.** If you think that your relationship is becoming less equitable, schedule a business meeting with your partner to discuss what you can do to get things feeling more balanced.

3. **Relationship roles.** If you find yourself focusing on aspects of your roles or your partner's roles that bother you, try to focus on what unique strengths these different roles bring to the relationship.

4. **Money.** Keeping an open conversation about finances is the best way to prevent money conflicts. Practice having conversations about spending, debt, savings, and money stories.

5. **Future planning.** Regular check-ins about your goals and what you're doing to accomplish them can prevent feelings of resentment or frustration when your relationship feels stagnant.

CHAPTER 3

Trust

Trust is one of the most fundamental pieces of a relationship. It's something we can't see but that is almost palpable in the way it is felt in a relationship. As they say, trust is earned, not given. Trust means we feel safe with our partner, emotionally and physically. Trust can be fostered through stability, vulnerability, consistency, honesty, openness, and some genuinely hard work. Trust is something that we may not come into a relationship with. We may have trauma, past relationships, or other life experiences that impacted our trust. But we can learn to trust again if we choose to work at it.

In this chapter, you will work through activities aimed at deepening your sense of trust and vulnerability. Exploring trust in your relationship may be hard for you, but it is well worth the effort.

I advise couples going through a major breach of trust, such as infidelity, any verbally or physically aggressive behavior, or chronic dishonesty, to work through some of those issues with a counselor before diving into this chapter.

ACTIVITY 1: What Is Your Attachment Style?

Our attachment style emerges from patterns we experienced in our childhood and usually sets the stage for how we behave in relationships. For example, a child with inconsistent caregivers might later struggle to feel safe in romantic relationships. Their childhood experiences taught them that people they love are not always there for them.

Attachment style can be adjusted, but it takes some hard work! Let's find out what your current attachment style is.

For each statement, circle the letter of the answer that best fits your situation.

1. Trusting my partner:

   a. Is relatively easy.

   b. Makes me feel anxious.

   c. Is sometimes easy and sometimes impossible.

   d. Is completely impossible.

2. When I first meet someone:

   a. It takes me some time to build trust, but I generally assume people are trustworthy.

   b. I'm unsure how they feel toward me, but I work hard to get them to like me. I might feel rejected if they don't show interest.

   c. It's hard for me to predict whether I can trust them, or I might trust them even though I feel they aren't good for me.

   d. They have to do a lot to earn my trust.

3. When it comes to commitments:

   a. I feel great making commitments with someone I love.

   b. I know I want a commitment, but being in it can make me worry.

   c. My needs for commitment tend to fluctuate.

   d. I don't usually like commitments to others.

4. When I look at my partnership:

   a. I think my partner and I love each other equally.

   b. I think I love my partner more than they love me.

   c. I feel like my partner sometimes hates me and sometimes loves me.

   d. I think my partner probably loves me more than I love them.

5. When I have to depend on my partner for something:

    a. I feel safe and trust that they'll do a good job.

    b. I worry that they might not like me depending on them for something.

    c. I expect to be let down. But I ask anyway.

    d. I realize that I can never rely on my partner for anything.

6. When it comes to being emotionally vulnerable with my partner:

    a. It comes naturally to me.

    b. I try to keep my feelings inside because I don't want to burden my partner.

    c. I might come off as dramatic or emotional because of my feelings.

    d. I find it is really hard.

7. When it comes to being physically intimate with my partner:

    a. It generally feels good!

    b. I want to be close with my partner, but I don't want to initiate often.

    c. I worry that my partner doesn't want to have sex with me or touch me. I struggle with feeling rejected.

    d. It's hard for me, and sometimes I come off as cold or distant.

8. If my partner behaved inappropriately toward me, like engaging in violence or doing something I identify as a dealbreaker:

    a. I'd feel comfortable leaving the relationship, though it may take some time and consideration.

    b. I might give my partner a lot of second chances.

    c. I'd feel like I deserved the inappropriate behavior.

    d. It would be very easy for me to walk away.

9. When my partner is angry:

    a. I'm able to remind myself that it's not about me; I don't feel their feelings.

    b. I might think that it's my fault.

    c. I may try to make them feel better.

    d. I ignore them until they're in a better space.

10. When I think about whether my partner and I might break up:

    a. I doubt my partner would ever initiate a breakup.

    b. I occasionally worry my partner might leave me.

    c. I constantly see signs that my partner will leave me.

    d. I feel like if anyone leaves the relationship, it will be me.

11. When I make decisions:

    a. I consider my partner's feelings, but they may not determine my choice.

    b. I perseverate on how my partner might feel in response to my decision.

    c. I might ask my partner to make the decision for me.

    d. I don't usually consider my partner's feelings.

RESULTS

Mostly a's, you may be *securely attached.*

Mostly b's, you may be *anxiously attached.*

Mostly c's, you may be *fearfully attached* (also known as having a disorganized attachment).

Mostly d's, you may be *avoidantly attached.*
Check out activity 2 to learn what these attachment terms mean!

Here's a little information about different attachment styles. Do you feel like the one you got in activity 1 fits for you?

	SECURE ATTACHMENT	ANXIOUS ATTACHMENT	FEARFUL/ DISORGANIZED ATTACHMENT	AVOIDANT ATTACHMENT
Overview	I'm okay; you're okay.	I'm not okay; you're okay.	I'm not okay; you're not okay.	I'm okay; you're not okay.
Emotional Closeness	I can be vulnerable	Being vulnerable might make me worry	If I'm vulnerable, I'll get hurt	I am not often vulnerable
Boundaries	Clear, healthy boundaries	Boundaries are weak or easily shifted	No boundaries	Rigid or extreme boundaries
Challenges	Trust is given and received easily	Relationships can cause anxiety; you may need a lot of reassurance from your partner.	Rejection is felt strongly, and you may feel dependent on the relationship; you might come off as "clingy"	The relationship may be a low priority; you may be perceived as being cold or distant.
Strengths	Relationships feel easy	The relationship is very important to you	Your partner's approval means a lot	You are independent
Childhood	Caregivers were consistent, emotionally available, and loving	Caregivers were less available or neglectful	Caregivers were unpredictable, violent, or confusing	Caregivers might have ignored the emotional needs of the child or might have been cold or distant

	SECURE ATTACHMENT	ANXIOUS ATTACHMENT	FEARFUL/ DISORGANIZED ATTACHMENT	AVOIDANT ATTACHMENT
Your Goal	Providing support to your partner if they have a different attachment style	Seeking less reassurance from your partner, building self-confidence and self-esteem	Fostering your own independence and self outside the relationship	Meeting your partner halfway, working on showing more love and warmth

ACTIVITY 3: **Attachment and Your Relationship**

What attachment style did you get in activity 1? Did it fit what you think of as your own attachment style?

Partner 1:

_____

Partner 2:

_____

Were you surprised by your partner's attachment style results? Was there anything in their attachment style description that surprised you?

Partner 1:

_____

_____

_____

Partner 2:

_____

_____

_____

What aspects of your attachment style seem to fit for you? What aspects don't?

Partner 1:

_____

_____

_____

Partner 2:

_____

_____

_____

How does your individual attachment style affect the relationship? Are there positive aspects of how your attachment impacts the partnership? Negative aspects? How does this affect your trust?

Partner 1:

_____

_____

_____

Partner 2:

_____

_____

_____

If you and your partner have different attachment styles, how can you "meet in the middle"?

Partner 1:

_____

_____

_____

Partner 2:

_____

_____

_____

What do you want to work on when it comes to attachment in your relationship?

Partner 1:

_____

_____

_____

Partner 2:

_____

_____

_____

Where do you think each of your attachment styles came from? Are there any childhood experiences or relationship traumas that might relate?

Partner 1:

_____

_____

_____

_____

Partner 2:

_____

_____

_____

_____

Even folks in the same partnership might have different ideas about what signifies a breach of trust. Use this checklist to see if you and your partner are on the same page. Some of these might seem obvious, and some might seem more abstract. Remember, everyone's idea of trust is different!

PARTNER 1 PARTNER 2

Partner 1	Partner 2	
☐	☐	Telling a white lie in order to protect your partner's feelings
☐	☐	Lying about where you've been
☐	☐	Purposefully not mentioning something that you know would hurt your partner's feelings or make them angry
☐	☐	Texting or emailing someone you find attractive
☐	☐	Connecting online with someone you've met in person and find attractive
☐	☐	Spending time with someone (other than your partner) who you've had sex with before
☐	☐	Breaking a promise
☐	☐	Standing up your partner
☐	☐	Drinking alcohol or using drugs without telling your partner
☐	☐	Talking to an ex regularly
☐	☐	Having sex with someone who isn't your partner
☐	☐	Making plans without your partner
☐	☐	Applying for a school or job without telling your partner
☐	☐	Being chronically late
☐	☐	Keeping feelings inside instead of expressing them to your partner
☐	☐	Not listening when your partner is telling you something
☐	☐	Not doing your part of household chores or other responsibilities
☐	☐	Quitting your job without talking to your partner
☐	☐	Having a "work wife"/"work husband"/"work partner"
☐	☐	Holding hands with someone to whom you are attracted

☐	☐	Having a crush without telling your partner
☐	☐	Yelling or screaming during arguments
☐	☐	Throwing items when you're upset
☐	☐	Making threats to your partner
☐	☐	Name-calling
☐	☐	Putting down or criticizing your partner
☐	☐	Making negative comments about your partner's friends or families
☐	☐	Making unsolicited comments about your partner's appearance or body
☐	☐	Stonewalling or purposefully evading conversations or topics
☐	☐	Criticizing your partner's sexual interests
☐	☐	Watching pornography
☐	☐	Fantasizing about someone other than your partner
☐	☐	Lying about being in a relationship
☐	☐	Speaking negatively about your partner to someone outside the relationship
☐	☐	Not wearing your wedding ring in public
☐	☐	Looking at your partner's messages, emails, or social media pages when they leave their phone out
☐	☐	Catching your partner in a lie about something mundane
☐	☐	Noticing when your partner is acting suspiciously
☐	☐	Threatening to break up with your partner
☐	☐	Not texting your partner back within a reasonable amount of time
☐	☐	Not hearing from your partner for a day or more
☐	☐	Borrowing or taking money from your partner or a shared bank account without telling them
☐	☐	Other:
☐	☐	Other:

ACTIVITY 5: Compare Your Ideas about Trust

Were your and your partners' results from the previous two activities more similar or more different than you'd anticipated?

_____

_____

What types of infidelity or trust-breaking situations have you experienced in past relationships? Do these experiences impact your trust of your current partner?

Partner 1:

_____

_____

_____

Partner 2:

_____

_____

_____

Are there any mutual areas of concerns around trust or fidelity?

_____

_____

_____

What do you and your partner agree are the three most significant breaches of trust listed in activity 4?

_____

_____

_____

What do you and your partner agree are the three least important breaches of trust listed in activity 4?

_____

_____

_____

Where do you feel like you learned messages about what are and are not breaches of trust in relationships: from the past? From relationships that were modeled to you, like those of friends or family? From TV or other media?

Partner 1:

_____

_____

_____

Partner 2:

_____

_____

_____

ACTIVITY 6: Types of Trust

Here are a few different types of trust in relationships. Which types are more or less challenging in your relationship?

TYPE OF TRUST	WHAT DOES IT MEAN?	WHY IS THIS IMPORTANT?	WHAT WOULD BE A BREACH OF TRUST?	HOW CAN YOU REPAIR THIS TYPE OF TRUST?
Sexual and Romantic Trust	Honoring your own and your partner's sexual and romantic boundaries	You and your partner have set sex and romance boundaries for a reason, and you trust each other to keep them. When you break this type of trust, you're showing your partner that you don't respect those boundaries.	Having sexual or romantic connections with others outside the relationship without your partner's consent	» Seeing a couples counselor together » Being fully open and honest » Being accountable for your actions » Remembering that healing and repair take time

TYPE OF TRUST	WHAT DOES IT MEAN?	WHY IS THIS IMPORTANT?	WHAT WOULD BE A BREACH OF TRUST?	HOW CAN YOU REPAIR THIS TYPE OF TRUST?
Emotional Trust	Trusting that your partner will hear your emotions without judgment, trusting that your partner will allow you to be vulnerable and will be vulnerable with you	Being in a relationship means you are the first person your partner comes to with their emotions. Your partner needs to feel safe sharing their emotions and know that you feel safe sharing yours.	Being hurtful or needlessly critical of your partner, using your partner's feelings to hurt them, being emotionally abusive in any way, refusing to be vulnerable with your partner, threatening your partner	» Seeking individual counseling for both partners » Making attempts to be vulnerable » Ceasing all emotionally abusive behavior immediately
Physical Trust	Being physically safe with your partner	Being physically safe with each other is necessary in having a healthy relationship. Violence is never okay.	Physically hurting your partner; using violence or aggression to intimidate or scare your partner, such as punching walls, throwing objects, or using your body in any way to make them feel unsafe.	» The physically aggressive partner needs to seek help to manage their aggression » The threatened partner should seek support on their own to regain their sense of safety » Only when individual work is done can the couple come together to repair the relationship

TYPE OF TRUST	WHAT DOES IT MEAN?	WHY IS THIS IMPORTANT?	WHAT WOULD BE A BREACH OF TRUST?	HOW CAN YOU REPAIR THIS TYPE OF TRUST?
Consistency	Being able to regulate your emotions and find stability in your feelings, behaviors, and choices	Stability is one of the pillars romantic love is built upon. Consistency is what helps you feel safe in relationships.	Behaving erratically, making impulsive choices, making decisions without thinking how they may affect your partner, refusing to address a mental illness that affects your day-to-day life	» If mental illness is getting in the way of your ability to regulate your emotions, seek counseling, either on your own or with your partner, to find ways to create safety in the relationship » Work on understanding each other's motivations, feelings, and thinking
Honesty	Telling the truth to each other	For any relationship to function, you need to know that you can trust what your partner says. Without honesty, you and your partner live in two very different realities.	Lying about big or little things, telling white lies, lying about what you're doing or who you're with, lying about your past	» Communicating with your partner about why you might be lying » Telling your partner when you feel tempted to lie » Telling your partner what feelings you might be trying to protect by lying » Seeking individual counseling to explore why you feel you need to hide something from your partner

TYPE OF TRUST	WHAT DOES IT MEAN?	WHY IS THIS IMPORTANT?	WHAT WOULD BE A BREACH OF TRUST?	HOW CAN YOU REPAIR THIS TYPE OF TRUST?
Something Else?				

ACTIVITY 7: Where Do We Need to Build Trust?

Part of being in a relationship means that you and your partner will certainly hurt each other from time to time. Breaches of trust happen. What types of trust have been broken in your past relationships?

PARTNER 1 PARTNER 2

☐	☐	Sexual and romantic trust
☐	☐	Emotional trust
☐	☐	Physical trust
☐	☐	Consistency
☐	☐	Honesty
☐	☐	Something else:

What areas of trust do you think you need to work on in your relationship? What breaches of trust have either of you participated in, if any?

PARTNER 1 PARTNER 2

☐	☐	Sexual and romantic trust
☐	☐	Emotional trust
☐	☐	Physical trust
☐	☐	Consistency
☐	☐	Honesty
☐	☐	Something else:

ACTIVITY 8: Repair Work

It's reasonable to assume that you and your partner have experienced some kind of breach of trust over the course of your relationship, whether it be something devastating or something more mundane.

Let's reflect on a specific trust-breaching experience for a moment. If you can't think of anything specific in your current relationship or you feel like it might be too tender of a topic, reflect back on a breach of trust you experienced in a past relationship or something you've seen in another relationship (a real-life relationship or something on TV or in a movie).

What happened? How did each person participate in the incident?

_____

_____

_____

_____

How was the breach of trust uncovered?

_____

_____

_____

What emotions did each of you experience during this incident?

Partner 1:

_____

Partner 2:

_____

What attempts did you make to repair your relationship after the incident? How did the responsible party seek forgiveness?

_____

_____

_____

How were the repair attempts received?

_____

_____

_____

Are there any ways you wish the responsible party had attempted to repair the relationship or seek forgiveness? How could they improve in the future?

_____

_____

_____

Did the breach of trust have any effects that continue to linger?

_____

_____

_____

_____

What will each of you commit to doing to continue to repair your relationship, forgive the other person, and address any lingering feelings about the breach of trust?

Partner 1:

_____

_____

_____

Partner 2:

_____

_____

_____

What causes us to break trust? This activity is an example of a "chain analysis," a tool from dialectical behavioral therapy (DBT) that helps us better understand why we act the way we do. This tool helps us take responsibility for our part of a problem. It's a good way to explore triggers, feelings, and emotions when trust has been broken.

This activity will help you develop a road map for what to do next time when you encounter a similar situation. Look at the different steps and fill in your own chart on a separate sheet of paper.

	EXAMPLE
What Happened?	I had a sexual encounter with someone other than my partner.
Vulnerabilities: What was going on that made you more likely to engage in the problem behavior?	
Prompting Event: What happened to lead you toward the problem behavior?	
Feeling Triggers: What emotions influenced your choice?	
Thought Triggers: What thoughts influenced your choice?	
Problem Behavior: What was the trust-breaking event?	
Short-Term Consequences: What short-term issues have come up since the event?	
Long-Term Consequences: What long-term issues have come up since the event?	

	EXAMPLE
Where I Could Have Changed Course: What could you have done differently?	
Plan: What do you plan to do differently if you're faced with the same triggers?	

ACTIVITY 10: The Trust You Have

The following is a list of actions that require trust and safety in a relationship. Check off the ones that you and your partner feel safe doing.

Some of these might feel basic to you and your partner, but you may find that you and your partner feel differently about these activities.

PARTNER 1   PARTNER 2

☐	☐	Holding hands
☐	☐	Making an apology
☐	☐	Admitting to something that you're not proud of
☐	☐	Having a heated argument
☐	☐	Telling a secret about yourself that you haven't told anyone before
☐	☐	Sustaining eye contact
☐	☐	Initiating sex with your partner
☐	☐	Crying in front of your partner
☐	☐	Expressing something you appreciate about your partner to them
☐	☐	Telling your partner about something you're interested in sexually
☐	☐	Asking for forgiveness
☐	☐	Admitting fault
☐	☐	Disagreeing with your partner
☐	☐	Confronting your partner about something they did that hurt your feelings

☐	☐	Sharing a song, book, or movie with your partner that's meaningful to you
☐	☐	Being open to a different perspective if you and your partner disagree
☐	☐	Being naked in front of your partner
☐	☐	Physical intimacy (outside of sex)
☐	☐	Public displays of affection
☐	☐	Admitting that you lied
☐	☐	Sharing feelings of insecurity
☐	☐	Saying "I love you"
☐	☐	Telling your partner something embarrassing about yourself
☐	☐	Telling your partner if you find someone else attractive
☐	☐	Introducing your partner to your family or friends
☐	☐	Taking your partner to a place that's special to you
☐	☐	Asking your partner for help when you need it
☐	☐	Communicating something you don't like about your sexual or physical intimacy
☐	☐	Telling your partner when you're going through a mental health challenge
☐	☐	Having a meaningful conversation about life, faith, beliefs, or values
☐	☐	Answering a difficult question about yourself
☐	☐	Complimenting your partner
☐	☐	Being complimented by your partner
☐	☐	Other:
☐	☐	Other:
☐	☐	Other:
☐	☐	Other:
☐	☐	Other:

ACTIVITY 11: What Do You Know?

How much do you really know about your partner? Try to guess how your partner would finish each of the following statements.

1. My partner's best friend is:

2. My partner's favorite book, movie, or TV show is:

3. If my partner could describe their childhood in one word, it would be:

4. My partner's favorite and least favorite family members are:

5. My partner's dream vacation is:

6. My partner's favorite weekend activity is:

7. My partner considers this person to be an inspiration or mentor:

8. My partner's dream job is:

9. If my partner could have any celebrity over to dinner, they'd invite:

10. My partner liked the following about me when we met:

11. A food my partner hates is:

12. The thing my partner is most afraid of is:

13. This is what my partner considers their biggest strength:

14. This is what my partner considers their biggest weakness:

Now have your partner review your answers and put a check mark next to those you got right.

If you got more statements right than wrong, good job! You know each other pretty well.

If you got more statements wrong than right, what do you think has kept you from knowing or learning these things about your partner?

If one of you guessed most of your partner's answers correctly but the other didn't, what has caused the inequity in emotional closeness? Does one of you ask more questions? Does one of you have better listening skills? What impact do you think this inequity might be having on your relationship?

ACTIVITY 12: Sharing Is Trust

In this activity, you'll give your partner ideas for experiences and activities you want to share with them. Some experiences will be ones you can share together; some of them will be things your partner will do on their own, like visit a restaurant you like or read a book you like.

Your goal as a couple is to complete everything on this list within the next year, as long as you consent.

	PARTNER 1'S CHOICES FOR PARTNER 2	PARTNER 2'S CHOICES FOR PARTNER 1
Media: a movie, TV show, or other visual media you want to share with them		
Learning: a book, concept, sport, or skill you want to share with them		
Places: a bar, restaurant, vacation spot, park, viewpoint, or house that is important to you that you want to show them		
Food: a special dish, cuisine, important recipe, or restaurant that is meaningful to you		
Activity: a day trip, museum, board game, craft, project, or class that sounds fun for you to do together		
Service: something you'd like them to do for you or help you ask for from your partner		
Person: someone important to you that you'd like them to meet		
Goal: a goal you hope your partner will achieve and you wish to support them in meeting		

ACTIVITY 13: Listening and Validating

Listening and validating are great skills for folks in relationships. Everyone wants to feel heard, and these skills can facilitate that.

Choose something you want to communicate to your partner. It could be an idea or a concern, or it could be something you appreciate. I recommend starting with something lighter before moving on to more serious things.

Now share what you want to say using the following steps. I've provided an example for each step, so you can see the kind of language to use.

LEVELS OF VALIDATION	YOUR GOAL	PROMPT	EXAMPLE
One	Being present	Give your partner your full attention	Facing your partner with comfortable eye contact, putting down phones or devices, turning off the TV as you speak
Two	Getting an accurate reflection	State exactly what you heard your partner say. Ask for clarity. Make sure you're understanding exactly what your partner is saying before moving on.	"I heard that you're feeling frustrated by that comment your boss made about you in front of your coworkers. Am I getting that right?"
Three	Learning to understand and predict your partner's feelings	Guess how your partner might be feeling based on what you know about them	"Based on what you've told me about how much you like and respect your boss, it must be especially hurtful for them to say that about you in front of your peers."

LEVELS OF VALIDATION	YOUR GOAL	PROMPT	EXAMPLE
Four	Tying in their history	Reflect on past experiences your partner has had that give the situation context	"I bet you're feeling pretty anxious about workplace dynamics because that was such a big area of stress about your last job."
Five	Normalizing	Validate your partner's emotions as a "normal" response that anyone in a similar situation might have	"I would be feeling worried about going back to work on Monday if that had happened to me."
Six	Radical genuineness	Share a common feeling or experience. Offer support or problem-solving help—if your partner wants it.	"This reminds me of my experience at my last job, where things like that happened all the time. I eventually felt like I had to leave the job. It was such a toxic dynamic. How can I support you in this?"

ACTIVITY 14: Steps to a Good Apology

Apologizing is another great skill that involves validation. Go through this practice with an experience that you and your partner have already worked through and apply it to a newer, more present concern.

	EXPLANATION	EXAMPLE
Step One: Validation	Go through the steps of validation to make sure that the partner who was hurt feels heard. We can't apologize authentically if we don't understand what we need to apologize for. Be open-minded; your partner might not be feeling exactly what you expect them to.	"It sounds like you're feeling hurt and angry because of how inappropriately I acted during our last argument. I said some mean things. I bet you were feeling scared, especially because of what you've experienced in past relationships. I might be feeling that way too if I were you. Am I getting that right?"
Step Two: Express remorse	Express a genuine apology. What exactly are you feeling remorseful for? What were you responsible for? This is not a good time to use any "buts," to give an explanation, or to be defensive.	"I behaved really inappropriately during our fight, and I feel so embarrassed. I don't like that I made you feel uncomfortable. I put you in a situation that made you feel scared, and I deeply apologize. I know that must have been horrible for you to go through."
Step Three: Make amends	What are you going to do differently? How will we make sure this doesn't happen again? What can we do to repair the trust that was broken by this action?	"I am going to work on my anger with a therapist. I don't like that side of myself, and I don't want to put you through that ever again. I'm going to work on walking away and taking breaks when I'm feeling too angry to talk."

	EXPLANATION	EXAMPLE
Step Four: Forgiveness	Now it's time to wait, to follow through on what you promised in the amend-making step, and to ask your partner what else they might need from you to forgive. Forgiveness takes time; you shouldn't expect that your partner is ready to forgive just because you're ready to apologize.	"Is there anything else you need from me? Do you have any suggestions for me on how I can work on my problem? I will look for a therapist today. I understand that you might need some time to think things over, so I will give you space. I don't need you to give me your forgiveness yet, and I'm here whenever you want to talk."

ACTIVITY 15: Emotional Intelligence

Emotional intimacy requires you to understand the emotions your partner might be feeling. This activity will help you gauge your levels of emotional intelligence.

Each of you can do this activity on your own. Then you can come together and compare your results.

Answer "true" or "false" for each of the following statements.

1. I generally know how I'm feeling and why I might be feeling that way.

2. I don't often lose my temper.

3. I know some ways to calm myself down when I become upset, and I use them.

4. Other people tell me I'm a good listener.

5. Sometimes I can predict what other people are feeling before they tell me.

6. When something small happens that negatively impacts my day, I'm able to turn things around and move on.

7. I'm able to hear others' feedback, opinions, or constructive criticism without becoming defensive or argumentative.

8. Having a difference of opinion with my partner is okay. We can have different perspectives and still get along.

9. I can usually read others' facial expressions or body language.

10. I'm able to stay relatively calm during stressful events.

11. I'm able to not take on others' emotions or feelings, even if they're very upset.

12. I use humor at appropriate times—to lighten the mood during stressful situations, for example.

13. I aim to see things from others' points of view, and I can shift my perspective.

14. I can see how my behaviors affect others.

15. I have tact; I can tell when it's an appropriate or inappropriate time to share certain things.

16. Others' emotions usually make some sense to me.

17. I can admit fault when I've made a mistake.

18. Friends and loved ones trust me to listen to them when things are difficult.

19. I feel able to voice concerns or grievances calmly and effectively.

20. I'm able to hear others express feelings without trying to fix them.

RESULTS

Mostly "true," you have strong emotional intelligence! You both can listen for others' emotions and handle your own.

Some "false," you can regard those statements as suggestions for where you may need to work on your emotional recognition skills.

Mostly "false," you may struggle to connect to others' emotions. This can be due to many different things—socialization, gender expectations, culture, social skills development, or even personality or biology. If you identify as neurodivergent, perhaps you have other strategies for recognizing others' emotions and connecting emotionally with others.

What Is Intelligence?

When they hear the word *intelligence,* most folks think of IQ, or the "intelligence quotient," and the IQ test, a standardized test that aims to measure a person's innate intellectual capabilities.

The IQ test has been criticized in recent years because it looks only at "practical," "rational," and Western ideas about what constitutes intelligence. Because it doesn't consider different cultural perspectives on intelligence, the IQ test is biased toward certain cultures or backgrounds. Plus, some question whether the IQ test actually measures what it says it does: intelligence and cognition.

Right now, IQ testing is considered, at best, an inefficient and reductive way of looking at human intelligence and, at worst, a colonizing and culturally biased approach toward evaluating what it means to be intelligent.

The emotional intelligence test in activity 15 provides a different take on intelligence. Had you considered emotional intelligence to be part of your overall intelligence? Which type of intelligence might be better suited to a successful marriage: traditional IQ or emotional intelligence?

ACTIVITY 16: Comfort in Intimacy

What are each of your goals for emotional closeness, trust, and intimacy? The following are some different intimacy "spectrums." I want you and your partner to each draw a vertical line on the spectrum, using different-colored pens or markers, to indicate where you feel comfortable with each type of intimacy.

How much do you like to share with your partner about what you're going through emotionally?

Not much   Some things   Everything

How do you feel about physical touch?

I don't like it.   I like it sometimes.   I crave it constantly.

How vulnerable and authentic are you with your partner?

| I keep my distance. | I show some things and hide others. | I want to be truly myself. |

How often would you prefer to communicate when you and your partner are not together?

| I like my space when we're not together. | Maybe a text here and there. | I like to be constantly in communication. |

I prefer relationships to be:

| Less serious | Somewhere in between | Very close |

How important is it that you and your partner have deep, meaningful conversations?

| Less important | Somewhere in between | Very important |

How much do you let your partner know about your life outside your marriage?

| Not much—I keep a lot inside. | Somewhere in between | I want them to know everything. |

If I'm upset:

| I try to hide my feelings. | I show some things and hide others. | My partner knows right away. |

If I haven't heard from my partner in a day:

| I wouldn't be concerned. | I might feel worried, depending on the situation. | This would feel weird to me. |

ACTIVITY 17: Building Emotional Intimacy

Here are some more opportunities to deepen your knowledge and understanding of your partner. For each statement, each partner has to share one thing that their partner doesn't know about them.

PARTNER 1 PARTNER 2

PARTNER 1	PARTNER 2	
☐	☐	Something we secretly disagree about
☐	☐	Something on my bucket list
☐	☐	A dream I've had
☐	☐	Something I've cried about
☐	☐	Something I do that drives you crazy (in a good way)
☐	☐	Something I do that drives you crazy (in a bad way)
☐	☐	A book or movie that affected me deeply
☐	☐	Something I'm thankful for
☐	☐	A prediction for the future
☐	☐	A nightmare I've had
☐	☐	Something strange that I believe in
☐	☐	A meaningful conversation I remember
☐	☐	Something stupid I did as a teenager
☐	☐	Something I've wanted us to do together that we haven't yet
☐	☐	Something that touched me emotionally
☐	☐	An emotion I feel is difficult to share
☐	☐	A time I've been angry
☐	☐	An ongoing worry I have
☐	☐	A guilty pleasure I'm actually embarrassed about
☐	☐	Something that defined me in my youth
☐	☐	A secret goal I haven't told you about
☐	☐	An insecurity I used to have
☐	☐	A happy memory from our time together
☐	☐	An important lesson I had to learn
☐	☐	A big mistake I made

		Something I think is hard about being a human
		A time I laughed until I cried
		A notable sexual experience

ACTIVITY 18: End-of-Chapter Check-In

How are you and your partner feeling about the emotional connection, trust, and safety in your relationship?

Partner 1:

_____

_____

_____

Partner 2:

_____

_____

_____

What was the most surprising thing you learned about your partner from this chapter? Was there anything that helped you see them or your relationship in a different light?

Partner 1:

_____

_____

_____

Partner 2:

_____

_____

_____

_____

Was this chapter easy or hard? Were there any difficult conversations? What were they, and how were you able to move on?

Partner 1:

_____

_____

_____

_____

_____

Partner 2:

_____

_____

_____

_____

_____

Where do you see opportunities to increase trust within your relationship? Is there anything you are ready to commit to today in order to further develop mutual trust in these areas?

Partner 1:

_____

_____

_____

_____

_____

Partner 2:

_____

_____

_____

_____

_____

Trust: Five Takeaways

1. **Attachment and closeness.** Your attachment style determines how comfortable you are being close and connected with others. While your attachment is something you pick up from early childhood experiences, you can always grow and change.

2. **Emotional intimacy.** Sharing and connecting with your partner are an important part of building trust. You can learn about your partner to deepen your closeness.

3. **Validation.** Validation is a communication skill that takes practice. Don't expect it to come naturally at first, but trust me, it will help your relationship.

4. **Defining trust.** Trust means many different things to different people and different couples. It's important for you and your partner to determine what trust means to you as a couple.

5. **When trust is broken.** Repairing a relationship after a breach of trust isn't a straightforward process, but it is worthwhile.

Trust: Five Conflict-Management Strategies

1. **Meet your partner where they are.** You chose your partner for a reason, and there are aspects of their personality that may not change. You may not always see eye to eye, but you can meet them where they are.

2. **Communication fosters connection.** The less you and your partner connect on a real, genuine level, the more chances there are for resentment and a lack of understanding to build up.

3. **Practice listening and validating.** Being present and truly hearing your partner is not a skill you're born with. You need to practice listening and validating your partner in order to become proficient at these skills.

4. **Expectations should be clear.** If you and your partner struggle with trust, your expectations for the relationship may be different. Review your expectations and boundaries frequently with your partner.

5. **Forgiveness takes time.** When trust is broken, forgiveness doesn't come overnight. Put in the work.

CHAPTER 4

Lifestyle and Career

think of our lifestyles as our different choices and preferences about how we live our lives, including the activities we enjoy, the foods we eat, the places we go, the jobs we work, and how we take care of our bodies.

Our lifestyle is dictated by many factors—our personality, habits, interests, tastes, and more. These factors can also influence our educational and career choices and determine how we manage our work–life balance. What we do in both our free time and our jobs sets the stage for who we are in our relationships.

Lifestyle factors can be huge areas of conflict in relationships. These aspects of your personhood and identity can cause friction in relationships if you and your partner have different wants, needs, or life goals. Let's figure out where you connect and where you may have some areas of challenge.

ACTIVITY 1: Checklist: Values

The way we live our lives is dictated in part by our values. Our values individuate us from others and help us foster a life path of growth and success that coincides with our passions and beliefs. A life without adherence to our values can make us feel unhappy, unfulfilled, and unchallenged.

What are your top 10 values? Give an item a check mark if you consider it to be a part of your value system. Make sure to choose only 10!

PARTNER 1	PARTNER 2		PARTNER 1	PARTNER 2	
☐	☐	Creativity	☐	☐	Ease
☐	☐	Compassion	☐	☐	Faith
☐	☐	Intellect	☐	☐	Social change

☐ ☐	Integrity		☐ ☐	Honesty
☐ ☐	Loyalty		☐ ☐	Experimentation
☐ ☐	Status		☐ ☐	Imagination
☐ ☐	Proximity		☐ ☐	Perfection
☐ ☐	Self-respect		☐ ☐	Relationships
☐ ☐	Power		☐ ☐	Passion
☐ ☐	Responsibility		☐ ☐	Cooperation
☐ ☐	Enjoyment		☐ ☐	Justice
☐ ☐	Cooperation		☐ ☐	Tangible skills
☐ ☐	Stability		☐ ☐	Playfulness
☐ ☐	Challenge		☐ ☐	Uplifting others
☐ ☐	Teamwork		☐ ☐	Sexual expression
☐ ☐	Consistency		☐ ☐	Education
☐ ☐	Adventure		☐ ☐	Physical ability
☐ ☐	Predictability		☐ ☐	Inspiration
☐ ☐	Financial security		☐ ☐	Expressiveness
☐ ☐	Community		☐ ☐	Understanding
☐ ☐	Excitement		☐ ☐	Open-mindedness
☐ ☐	Sustainability		☐ ☐	Other:
☐ ☐	Novelty		☐ ☐	Other:
☐ ☐	Innovation		☐ ☐	Other:
☐ ☐	Efficiency		☐ ☐	Other:
☐ ☐	Leadership		☐ ☐	Other:
☐ ☐	Fame		☐ ☐	Other:
☐ ☐	Technology		☐ ☐	Other:
☐ ☐	Risk		☐ ☐	Other:
☐ ☐	Commitment to learning		☐ ☐	Other:
☐ ☐	Optimization		☐ ☐	Other:
☐ ☐	Expertise			

From the top 10 values you identified in activity 1, what would you select as your top three? Of those, what's your number one?

Partner 1:

_____

_____

_____

Partner 2:

_____

_____

_____

Did you and your partner differ in the values you selected as most important? Did anything surprise you?

_____

_____

_____

Does your current career, job, or daily work represent the values you indicated were the most important to you? What aspects of your current work do or don't align with your value system?

Partner 1:

_____

_____

_____

Partner 2:

_____

_____

_____

Would you be willing to sacrifice one or more of the top 10 values in your career if it meant you got your number one or even your top three?

Partner 1:

_____

_____

_____

Partner 2:

_____

_____

_____

Have you or your partner ever had a job with values that were vastly different from your individual value system? What happened? How did that affect your personal and professional life?

_____

_____

_____

_____

_____

_____

How do your top three values show up in your personal life?

_____

_____

_____

As a couple, what do you think might happen if partners aren't able to live in congruence with their values, whether it be in their personal or professional worlds?

_____

_____

_____

ACTIVITY 3: Career Satisfaction

Does your happiness at work affect your marriage? Start by taking this quiz to determine how happy you are in your current position, regardless of what kind of job you do.

For each statement, answer one of the following:

a. Mostly true

b. Sometimes true

c. Never true

1. Doing my job brings me joy.

2. I feel excited talking about my work with others.

3. I am happy to get feedback about how I can perform my job better.

4. I enjoy working alongside my colleagues.

5. I feel like my job is well suited to my personality, interests, and abilities.

6. If something difficult happens at work, I'm able to bounce back quickly.

7. Things that happen at work rarely impact my personal life.

8. I wake up excited to go into my job or perform my duties.

9. I'm able to be true to myself and my beliefs in my workplace.

10. My work serves a purpose that is important to me.

11. The work I do is in line with my life goals.

RESULTS

Mostly a's, it sounds like you've found a career or role that fits very well with your beliefs and values. You are happy to be doing what you're doing, feel that there is greater purpose in your work, and are well suited for your career. Your relationship probably isn't affected by your career satisfaction.

Mostly b's, your career might not be a total match for you. Your values might not sync up with your roles and responsibilities, or maybe your job environment is not as safe and comfortable as you'd like. It might be a good time to start considering a career change or to redefine your role for yourself. Your feelings about your career might be starting to impact the relationship.

Mostly c's, your work is not working for you, and it's likely harming your relationship. You don't feel like you're very good at your job or don't like what you're doing. Consider things you could do to improve your career outlook.

ACTIVITY 4: Career Goals

What goals do you have for your career? Are all your goals for your career being met by your current job or role? Put a check mark beside the goals that you think could be met in your current position. Put an X beside goals that you think are not achievable in your current role.

PARTNER 1 PARTNER 2

☐	☐	Make more money
☐	☐	Make an impact on a large scale
☐	☐	Spend less time at work
☐	☐	Work from home
☐	☐	Travel for work
☐	☐	Have more freedom in your career
☐	☐	Pursue more education
☐	☐	Work for a cause you believe in
☐	☐	Feel more challenged
☐	☐	Gain responsibility
☐	☐	Have peers you like at work
☐	☐	Improve work–life balance
☐	☐	Feel like your work represents you
☐	☐	Work fewer hours
☐	☐	Connect with like-minded colleagues
☐	☐	Learn a new skill or trade
☐	☐	Feel more confident in your career
☐	☐	Feel like an expert in your field
☐	☐	Advance your field
☐	☐	Have more freedom and autonomy in your role
☐	☐	Find your passion

☐	☐	Work more hours
☐	☐	Feel a deep connection to your work
☐	☐	Increase your performance
☐	☐	Be your own boss
☐	☐	Improve your efficiency
☐	☐	Start a business
☐	☐	Network
☐	☐	Have a more flexible work schedule
☐	☐	Be able to leave work at work
☐	☐	Have a collaborative work environment
☐	☐	Manage others
☐	☐	Feel less challenged
☐	☐	Have more structure at your job
☐	☐	Feel happier at work
☐	☐	Feel like your personality aligns with your workplace
☐	☐	Be more productive
☐	☐	Feel appreciated in your role
☐	☐	Have benefits with your job that are important to you
☐	☐	Have a casual workplace
☐	☐	Utilize your individual strengths
☐	☐	Other:
☐	☐	Other:
☐	☐	Other:
☐	☐	Other:
☐	☐	Other:

ACTIVITY 5: Career Exploration

Are there aspects of your career that don't align with your values? Does your current job support your overall goals? What doesn't align?

Partner 1:

_____

_____

_____

Partner 2:

_____

_____

_____

What changes do you think you need to make in order to reach a better place with your career?

Partner 1:

_____

_____

_____

Partner 2:

_____

_____

_____

What impact do you feel your career has on your life and relationship?

Partner 1:

_____

_____

_____

Partner 2:

_____

_____

_____

What do you think would make your partner happier in their career? What other steps do you think they could take in order to have a career that aligns with their beliefs and values?

Partner 1:

_____

_____

_____

Partner 2:

_____

_____

_____

ACTIVITY 6: Career Goals

Let's talk career goals! Start by making each of your goals "SMART":

S: Specific goals are clear and direct. For example, if your goal is to "make more money," do you hope for a specific salary? Or do you hope to start a side business? Find a new job? If so, in what?

M: Measurable goals mean we can review progress and see how you're doing. If your goal is to "work less," does that mean fewer than 40 hours a week? Fewer than 80 hours a week? Not at all?

A: Attainable goals are realistic and achievable. Becoming your own boss by next Tuesday is probably not realistic. Becoming your own boss in five years may be more attainable.

R: Relevant career goals are ones that are important to you and your personal passions. They are meaningful and represent more than just a goal. For a therapist like me, a relevant goal might be to serve a new population of patients. A less relevant career goal might be learning how to code.

T: Timebound goals have a specific due date. The following chart will help you attach time frames to your goals. You should have different goals for each time frame.

How can you break down big goals into SMART steps? If your goal is to go back to school, what do you need to do in the next month, six months, a year, the years to come? You might research schools, apply for programs, relocate if necessary, and so on. Depending on your age, for goals 10 to 40 years out, it might be a good idea to start thinking about retirement or other end-of-life plans.

	PARTNER 1	PARTNER 2
1 MONTH		
6 MONTHS		
1 YEAR		
2 YEARS		
5 YEARS		
10 YEARS		

Some of the biggest things I see couples argue about are lifestyle factors and living preferences. Perhaps one partner is a yoga fanatic who drinks green juices and the other is a dive bar–loving video gamer. It doesn't matter how much they love each other; they might have some challenges when it comes to what they actually do together.

The following is a list of different lifestyle factors. Put a check mark beside those you're happy to have in your life. Leave a blank next to things you'd prefer not to have in your life.

PARTNER 1	PARTNER 2	
☐	☐	Exercising
☐	☐	Living with family
☐	☐	Drinking alcohol
☐	☐	Eating healthy
☐	☐	Being vegetarian or vegan
☐	☐	Living with roommates
☐	☐	Living outside your hometown
☐	☐	Moving for work
☐	☐	Hobbies
☐	☐	Using recreational drugs
☐	☐	Having sex
☐	☐	Living in the suburbs
☐	☐	Keeping a clean house
☐	☐	Being organized
☐	☐	Having close friends
☐	☐	Spending time with family
☐	☐	Living in a rural area
☐	☐	Working a traditional job
☐	☐	Working a nontraditional job
☐	☐	Monogamy
☐	☐	Non-monogamy

☐	☐	Smoking cigarettes
☐	☐	Staying at home
☐	☐	Practicing religious or spiritual traditions
☐	☐	Open and honest communication
☐	☐	Living in a city
☐	☐	Being vulnerable
☐	☐	Self-growth
☐	☐	Luxury items
☐	☐	Travel
☐	☐	Other:
☐	☐	Other:
☐	☐	Other:

ACTIVITY 8: Lifestyle Factors Review

What lifestyle factors do you and your partner agree are important?

_____

_____

_____

How important are these factors to you as a couple?

_____

_____

Were there any factors that both of you checked that are not present in the relationship? For example, maybe both of you marked exercise as being important, but you haven't been to the gym in a long while.

_____

_____

_____

What do you think has gotten in the way of you and your partner incorporating these factors into your life together?

_____

_____

_____

_____

How do you plan to make these missing factors a priority for you?

_____

_____

_____

_____

What lifestyle factors did you and your partner have a difference of opinion about?

_____

_____

_____

_____

How important to each of you are the factors you disagreed about?

_____

_____

_____

_____

How have you and your partner been able to negotiate around these differences?

_____

_____

_____

Have you and your partner ever had any conflicts related to these differences in lifestyle factors? How did you manage the conflict? What did you learn?

_____

_____

_____

Does this conflict feel resolved? Or are there lingering feelings that may need to be addressed?

_____

_____

_____

Are any of these factors you disagree about nonnegotiable for either of you?

_____

_____

_____

Is this factor a dealbreaker in the relationship? If not, what kind of an agreement can you make?

_____

_____

_____

ACTIVITY 9: Lifestyle Happiness

Does your lifestyle fit with your beliefs, values, and goals? Are you doing what you think you should be doing with your life? Let's find out.

For each statement, answer one of the following:

a. Mostly true

b. Sometimes true

c. Rarely true

1. I am doing what I feel like I should be doing with my life.

2. I feel good about the choices I make.

3. I am where I feel like I should be in my life.

4. I live a good life.

5. I do the things that I want to do.

6. I feel as though my partner and I are working toward the same goals.

7. My behaviors represent who I am as a person.

8. I feel fulfilled by the things I do and the choices I make.

9. I am working toward something that is important to me.

10. I practice skills, talents, or hobbies that are important to me in my spare time.

11. I don't often feel shame or regret for things I do.

12. I feel like my partner is able to see who I truly am.

13. The people I know would say I am living in accordance with my values and personality.

14. My relationships with others are meaningful and genuine.

RESULTS

Mostly a's, you're probably living a life that fits with your overall lifestyle goals. Your personality and self are present in what you do. Your choices don't feel in conflict with who you are.

Mostly b's, there are aspects of your life where you live in accordance with your values, but there are things you do that don't feel like you. What's getting in the way of you living the life you want?

Mostly c's, there's a lot of dissonance between who you want to be and who you are today. This could be for a variety of reasons. Maybe the reality of life prevents you from doing the things you love and being the person you want to be. What choices can you make, regardless of how small, to feel as though you're living a life more congruent with yourself?

Ikigai is a Japanese word for "a reason for being," or the meaning for your life. We are all searching for our ikigai, and it can take us our entire lives to find it. Seeking purpose is not an easy task, but it can have benefits in our career, our personal well-being, and our relationships.

This visual explanation of ikigai (originally appearing in Andres Zuzunaga's work) can help you understand what seeking your ikigai might entail.

What you love
to do

Passion   Mission

What you're   Ikigai   What the
good at   world needs

Profession   Vocation

What you can
be paid for

ACTIVITY 11: Ikigai Exploration

Using the graphic from activity 10, let's explore your and your partner's ikigai.

	EXAMPLE	PARTNER 1	PARTNER 2
What You Love to Do: tasks, hobbies, jobs, or work that you enjoy doing	Designing spaces, being creative		
What the World Needs: valuable skills, ideas, or solutions you see as necessary for societal growth	Helping in managing their lives		
What You Can Be Paid For: things you can do that could, in some way, make you money	Working with people one-on-one		
What You're Good At: your strengths, abilities, talents, or skills	Connecting with people		
Your Mission: what you love and find fulfilling plus what the world needs	Being a personal assistant		

	EXAMPLE	PARTNER 1	PARTNER 2
Your Vocation: what the world needs plus what you can be paid for	Being a coach		
Your Profession: what you can be paid for plus what you're good at	Being a social worker		
Your Passion: what you're good at plus what you love	Being an interior designer		
Your Ikigai: putting it all together	Being a professional organizer!		

What did you discover about yourself in the ikigai activity?

Partner 1:

_____

_____

_____

Partner 2:

_____

_____

_____

Was there anything you learned about your partner?

Partner 1:

_____

_____

_____

Partner 2:

_____

_____

_____

Looking at your current career and lifestyle, do you feel like it fits into your sense of ikigai?

Partner 1:

_____

_____

_____

Partner 2:

_____

_____

_____

What do you feel is lacking in your life or profession when it comes to a sense of ikigai?

Partner 1:

_____

_____

_____

Partner 2:

_____

_____

_____

What changes do you need to make to your career or lifestyle in order to live out your ikigai more fully?

Partner 1:

_____

_____

_____

Partner 2:

_____

_____

_____

ACTIVITY 13: Current Lifestyle

What does your current lifestyle look like? What are things you find yourselves doing on a regular basis? Let's make a calendar of your daily tasks and activities for an average week.

Try and make the calendar as accurate as possible. In the next activity, you'll consider what changes you'd like to make to it.

	EXAMPLE	PARTNER 1	PARTNER 2
SUNDAY	Do chores, prep meals, grocery shop, take the dogs for a walk		
MONDAY	Work 9 to 5, make dinner, go to the gym		
TUESDAY	Work 9 to 5, take the dogs for a walk, do the dishes		
WEDNESDAY	Work 9 to 5, run errands, have a date night		
THURSDAY	Work from home, take the dogs for a walk, go to therapy, clean the house, run errands, go to class		

	EXAMPLE	PARTNER 1	PARTNER 2
FRIDAY	Work 9 to 5, hang out with friends		
SATURDAY	Clean the house, go for a hike, spend time with family		

ACTIVITY 14: Lifestyle Dreams

If you could have the most perfect lifestyle you could ever imagine, what would it look like? How is it similar to your current schedule? How is it different? Do you and your partner's dream schedules align?

	EXAMPLE	PARTNER 1	PARTNER 2
SUNDAY	Go to the gym, take a leisurely walk, have a nice potluck dinner with friends		
MONDAY	Work 9 to 2, go to the gym, take the dogs for a walk, make dinner		

	EXAMPLE	PARTNER 1	PARTNER 2
TUESDAY	Work 9 to 2, go to the gym, take the dogs for a walk, meet friends for drinks		
WEDNESDAY	Work 9 to 2, go to the gym, take the dogs for a walk, make dinner, watch a movie with my partner		
THURSDAY	Work from home, go to the gym, take the dogs for a walk, have a date night with my partner		
FRIDAY	Take the day off, go on a short day trip with the dogs, come back home and work from home in the early evening, spend time with friends and family		
SATURDAY	Clean the house, go for a hike, spend leisure time with family		

Before you turn your relationship and life upside down trying to meet your dream lifestyle, let's take a closer look at the priorities behind your weekly lifestyle goals.

Following is a list of 22 different lifestyle factors. Feel free to add your own, unique-to-you factors at the end, if needed. Then rank the factors in order of importance to you, with 1 being the most important. The number one factor is something you'd like to do every week.

PARTNER 1 PARTNER 2

		Spending time with my partner
		Spending time with my family
		Spending time with my friends
		Advancing my career
		Continuing education/learning a new skill
		Keeping a clean house
		Taking care of children's/pets' needs
		Eating healthy
		Exercising
		Having leisure time or alone time
		Having sex
		Participating in spiritual/faith activities
		Reading
		Working on projects
		Helping others
		Working toward goals
		Working on a hobby
		Other:
		Other:
		Other:

ACTIVITY 16: Compatibility

Let's see if you and your partner share similar needs for space, activity, and social interaction.

1. Your ideal vacation:

    a. Somewhere tropical and relaxing

    b. A staycation at home

    c. Backpacking in a new country

2. A perfect day off:

    a. Relaxing at home and then spending time with friends and family

    b. Working on a home project, reading, or watching a movie together

    c. Taking a day trip to a new place

3. Your need for space:

    a. I like spending time with friends and family, but I also need my alone time.

    b. I am more introverted and prefer to spend time by myself or only with my partner.

    c. I feel best when I'm surrounded by friends or family.

4. If your partner was planning a birthday celebration for you, it would be:

    a. A low-key night out with some close friends

    b. A quiet dinner together

    c. An all-night rager with all our friends

5. How do you think of yourself socially?

    a. Easygoing, go with the flow

    b. Quiet, reserved, sensitive

    c. Gregarious, spontaneous

6. Your favorite social attribute of your partner:

  a. They're laid-back and open to new things.

  b. They need their quiet time too.

  c. They're always up for an adventure.

7. When we spend time apart:

  a. I'm usually spending time with friends doing a group hobby or activity I love.

  b. I'm doing something independent on my own, like playing a video game or working on a creative project.

  c. I'm out having a wild night with some friends.

8. What's the most important part of the relationship?

  a. Getting along

  b. Having our own space

  c. Having fun

RESULTS

Mostly a's, you're a medium-stimulus person. You might identify as an "ambivert," someone who's riding the line between introversion and extroversion. You're relatively go with the flow when it comes to social situations—you would be happy to be at a fun kickback or holed up on the couch during a Netflix marathon. You can usually keep up with an extrovert or enjoy the quieter demeanor of an introvert.

Mostly b's, you're a lower-stimulus person. You identify as an introvert and might need space and time to recharge if you're around others. Your favorite hobbies may be ones that you do on your own. You would get on well with introverts or ambiverts. If you're married to an extrovert, you and your partner might need to do some negotiating about how you spend your couple time.

Mostly c's, you're a high-stimulus person, also known as an extrovert. You feel the most alive when you're with a big group of people, doing something exciting, novel, or new. You likely get on very well with extroverts or ambiverts. Challenges might come up between an extrovert and an introvert—your energy might be too much for them. But who knows? Opposites can attract!

Love Languages

Dr. Gary Chapman's book *The 5 Love Languages* came from his decades of research on the ways people give and receive love. He identified five primary love languages:

Physical Touch   **Gift Giving**

Words of Affirmation   **Acts of Service**

Quality Time

You may be able to speak all of these love languages, or you may have a few that you can speak better than the others. Sometimes your partner's style of giving or receiving love may be in conflict with your manner of giving or receiving love, which can lead one or both of you to feel unappreciated or unheard.

It's important to know the ways you and your partner prefer to give and receive love so that you can best communicate and understand the appreciation you have for each other.

ACTIVITY 17: Love Language Survey

Check the ways you like to show your partner that you love them. The category that has the most check marks is probably the language you're most fluent in.

PHYSICAL TOUCH

PARTNER 1 PARTNER 2

☐	☐	Spending time cuddling on the couch
☐	☐	Holding your hand in public
☐	☐	Giving you a hug
☐	☐	Sitting close to you
☐	☐	Giving you a back scratch

WORDS OF AFFIRMATION

PARTNER 1 PARTNER 2

☐	☐	Saying "I love you"

☐	☐	Telling you why they appreciate you
☐	☐	Sharing memories together
☐	☐	Giving you compliments
☐	☐	Talking you up to their friends or family

QUALITY TIME

PARTNER 1 PARTNER 2

☐	☐	Running errands together
☐	☐	Binging a new series together
☐	☐	Going on regular dates
☐	☐	Spending one-on-one time together
☐	☐	Planning a fun activity for you two to do alone

GIFT GIVING

PARTNER 1 PARTNER 2

☐	☐	Picking you up your favorite snack at the grocery store
☐	☐	Buying you something "just because"
☐	☐	Getting you something that you've had your eye on for a while
☐	☐	Buying flowers or other little thoughtful gifts
☐	☐	Saving up for a very special gift

ACTS OF SERVICE

PARTNER 1 PARTNER 2

☐	☐	Doing a chore they know you don't like
☐	☐	Making you meals
☐	☐	Cleaning the house
☐	☐	Paying the bills
☐	☐	Taking care of the kids or pets

ACTIVITY 18: How Alike Are You?

So far, in this chapter, we've gone through many different lifestyle, personality, and work factors that can impact your relationship. I'm sure that you and your partner have found many ways that you're alike and many ways that you're different. On the following spectrums, put a vertical line where you think you and your partner are on each spectrum.

How important is work to you?

Not that important   In the middle   Very important

How important is time with friends and family?

Not that important   In the middle   Very important

How much time should you and your partner spend together?

I prefer more   Somewhere   I like to spend
independence.   in the middle   time together.

Are you an introvert or extrovert?

Introvert   Ambivert   Extrovert

How happy do you feel in your career?

Very happy   Somewhere in the middle   Very unhappy

Do you feel like your career lines up with your values and beliefs?

Yes   Somewhere in between   No

Do you feel like you have a purpose or meaning in life?

Yes   Maybe   No

Does your partner show love in a language you can understand?

Yes   Maybe   No

End-of-Chapter Check-In

After going through all the activities in this chapter, are you and your partner more alike or more different than you anticipated? What were the biggest differences?

_____

_____

_____

What do these differences mean to your relationship? How can you leverage these differences to build a stronger bond?

_____

_____

_____

Were there any things that you had thought of as dealbreakers? What perspective do you have on these differences now?

_____

_____

_____

_____

What did you learn about your partner's love languages?

Partner 1:

_____

_____

_____

Partner 2:

_____

_____

_____

Lifestyle and Career: Five Takeaways

1. **Values.** Your beliefs and values are part of how you look at life. It's important for you to have at least some values in common with your partner!

2. **Career satisfaction.** Your happiness in your career does have an impact on your relationship. Marriage satisfaction is, in part, related to how you feel about what you do.

3. **Life purpose.** Your life's purpose, or ikigai, is not necessarily easy to find. But finding purpose allows you to feel fulfillment not only in your career but also in other facets of your life, including your marriage.

4. **Lifestyle.** Lifestyle refers to what you do in your life—your hobbies, your interests, and your work. It includes the day-by-day factors that affect your relationship!

5. **Love languages.** It's crucial to know how your partner best shows and receives love. The way you show love is the most important way that you communicate in marriage.

Lifestyle and Career: Five Conflict-Management Strategies

1. **Explore different values without judgment.** Not every couple is going to share the same values, but understanding and accepting what your partner values and why is important for your relationship.

2. **When your job sucks.** It's likely that there will come a time when you or your partner has a job that they don't enjoy. Be encouraging and supportive, but set boundaries to prevent yourself from trying to fix the problem.

3. **Find meaning.** Purpose is not an easy thing to find. If you and your partner feel stuck in a rut, return to your ikigai chart to see if something's missing.

4. **Meet in the middle.** It's important to understand your partner's lifestyle needs and compromise so that both of you can get your needs met.

5. **Ask your partner to speak your love language.** If you and your partner show or receive love in different ways, ask your partner to show love in the way that you can best receive it.

CHAPTER 5

Physical Intimacy and Sexuality

n this chapter, we'll discuss one of the more heated areas of relationship work: sex. For most couples, sexuality is what makes marriage different than other relationships in their life. Yet it's something that most partners struggle to communicate about.

Maybe your sexual relationship connected you at first, or perhaps you've explored only recently. Maybe things started off hot and heavy, and now they've cooled. Or you feel like you're out of the groove.

I find that couples worry when their sex isn't going well or they're going through a sexual lull. They wonder if it indicates that there may be more serious issues they need to address. It is my belief that sexual challenges in relationships represent a lack of connection, but not one that is unsolvable. That connection can absolutely be rebuilt.

ACTIVITY 1: Talking about Sex

Our culture has set us up for limited conversations about sex and sexuality. The values inherent in our culture and media can make us feel uncomfortable in talking about something that is so normal and natural and a part of being a human being with a body.

Let's assess your comfort level. Put a check mark beside each topic that you feel comfortable talking about with your partner. Remember not to judge if there's something your partner isn't ready to talk about yet.

☐	☐	Sexually transmitted infection (STI) history
☐	☐	Birth control and safe sex
☐	☐	Past sexual partners
☐	☐	Things you like that your partner does
☐	☐	Things you dislike that your partner does
☐	☐	Fantasies involving your partner
☐	☐	Kinks
☐	☐	Things you're interested in exploring
☐	☐	Sexual boundaries and hard limits
☐	☐	What sexual touch and pleasure feel like to you
☐	☐	Sexual trauma, abuse, or assault
☐	☐	Nonsexual physical intimacy
☐	☐	Things you want your partner to do to you
☐	☐	Things you want to do to your partner
☐	☐	Monogamy/non-monogamy
☐	☐	Fantasies about people who aren't your partner
☐	☐	Pornography
☐	☐	Menstruation
☐	☐	Desire
☐	☐	Awkward sexual moments
☐	☐	Bodily fluids
☐	☐	Sex drive/libido
☐	☐	Things that have made you laugh during sex
☐	☐	Your level of sexual satisfaction in the relationship
☐	☐	Sex toys
☐	☐	Foreplay
☐	☐	Your experience of arousal
☐	☐	Masturbation
☐	☐	Abstinence

☐	☐	Orgasm
☐	☐	Inorgasmia (inability to orgasm)
☐	☐	Giving sexual consent or saying no
☐	☐	Sexuality and faith
☐	☐	Gender identity/dysphoria
☐	☐	Sexual shame
☐	☐	Our sexual routine
☐	☐	Pain or discomfort during or after sex
☐	☐	Sexual orientation

ACTIVITY 2: Sexual Communication Assessment

Based on the previous activity, what topics are you most excited to discuss with your partner?

Partner 1:

_____

_____

_____

_____

Partner 2:

_____

_____

_____

_____

What topics did both you and your partner not want to talk about?

_____

_____

_____

_____

Why did you not want to discuss these topics?

Partner 1:

_____

_____

Partner 2:

_____

_____

If discussions in this chapter bring up any feelings of discomfort, how can you communicate that to your partner?

Partner 1:

_____

_____

Partner 2:

_____

_____

How can your partner support you if these uncomfortable feelings emerge?

Partner 1:

_____

_____

Partner 2:

_____

_____

Is there anything you think is important for your partner to know about your sexual history or orientation?

Partner 1:

_____

_____

Partner 2:

_____

_____

| ACTIVITY 3: **What Do We Do?** |

Let's see what you and your partner's physical intimacy and sexuality look like. Before starting this activity, determine whether you and your partner would like to limit the discussion to things you've done together or if you're open to discussing things you've tried in past relationships. Also, remember to be mindful of topics you agreed not to discuss yet.

In the following list of activities, write "1" next to something that you and/or your partner do or have done regularly. Write "2" next to things you and/or your partner have tried once or twice. Feel free to add items at the end.

PARTNER 1   PARTNER 2

Holding hands

Hugging

Kissing

Putting your arm around your partner

Public displays of affection

Giving/receiving a massage

Using dirty talk

Stripping or dancing for your partner

Visiting a strip club together

Sending/receiving nudes or sexual photos or videos

Making a sexual photo or video together

Watching porn together

Showing your partner something you like in porn

Giving/receiving manual stimulation

Giving/receiving oral sex

Giving/receiving vaginal penetration

Giving/receiving anal penetration

_____	_____	Giving/receiving analingus
_____	_____	Teasing/being teased by your partner
_____	_____	Having "rough" sex
_____	_____	Playing a dominant role
_____	_____	Playing a submissive role
_____	_____	Using toys during sex
_____	_____	Public sex
_____	_____	Mutual masturbation
_____	_____	Masturbating in front of your partner
_____	_____	Double penetration
_____	_____	Inviting another person or more to participate in sexual acts
_____	_____	Wearing lingerie or sexual costumes during sex
_____	_____	Romantic sex (making love)
_____	_____	Passionate sex
_____	_____	Maintenance sex
_____	_____	Kinky sex
_____	_____	Spanking or being spanked
_____	_____	"69"ing
_____	_____	Role-playing during sex
_____	_____	Visiting a sex club or orgy
_____	_____	Other: _____
_____	_____	Other: _____

Now, review each other's responses. Discuss which activities you are interested in trying and which activities you are not interested in.

ACTIVITY 4: Your Sexual Script

You sexual script is the typical "routine" that you and your partner work through when you're physically intimate.

Our sexual scripts are often informed by our culture. For example, our culture tells us that heterosexual, cisgender men are expected to be the aggressor and initiate sex. We see this stereotype in movies, in some pornography, and in literature, and it's often perpetuated by the way we discuss sexuality with our friends, family, and partners. This script has become a "norm" in many relationships.

All couples have set scripts that are made up of these norms as well as the routine that has emerged in your relationship. This version of Mad Libs will help you see what your script is.

_____ *usually initiates sex by*
        PERSON

_____ .
        ACTION

Usually this occurs in the _____ .
                                        PLACE

The first sexual act we engage in is _____ ,
                                        SEXUAL BEHAVIOR

which is then usually followed by _____ .
                                        SEXUAL BEHAVIOR

The "main event" of our sexual routine is _____ .
                                        SEXUAL BEHAVIOR

During sex, **none / one / both partner(s)** *usually orgasm during*
                        CIRCLE ONE

_____ / _____ .
        SEXUAL BEHAVIOR   SEXUAL BEHAVIOR

We know sex is over when _____ .
                            ACTION/FEELING/EXPERIENCE

After sex, we _____ .
                ACTION/FEELING/EXPERIENCE

ACTIVITY 5: Your Frequency

How frequently are you and your partner physically and sexually intimate? Looking at the past week, record when you and your partner engaged in sexual behavior or physical intimacy—and what kind.

	EXAMPLE	SEXUAL BEHAVIOR
SUNDAY	Snuggled on the couch and watched TV, had oral sex	
MONDAY	Gave each other a hug and kiss before and after work	
TUESDAY	Gave each other a hug and kiss before and after work	
WEDNESDAY	Gave each other a hug and kiss before and after work, watched TV and snuggled on the couch	
THURSDAY	Went to a concert, danced, had penetrative sex	

	EXAMPLE	SEXUAL BEHAVIOR
FRIDAY	Gave each other a hug and kiss before and after work	
SATURDAY	Had sex in the morning, held hands on a walk, fell asleep cuddling	

Is Everyone Having More Sex Than We Are?

Studies show that virtually everyone thinks that other people are having more sex than they are. Research done by the National Center for Health Statistics shows that our sexual debut, our number of sexual partners, and the frequency of our sexual acts are more different than what we'd expect.

This study showed that by age 19, around 68 percent of teens have experienced their sexual debut, or their first sexual relation. This means that more than 30 percent of Americans had not had a sexual experience until their 20s.

It also showed that 73 percent of all folks between the ages of 25 and 44 only had one opposite-sex partner in the previous year. Folks with same-sex partners accounted for 5 percent of men and 11 percent of women of that sample. Only 14 percent of men and 6 percent of women had multiple opposite-sex partners.

The most interesting of all these statistics was the question of frequency: How many times a year does the average American have sex? The answer is an average of 60 times a year, so just over once per week.

ACTIVITY 6: Desire Calendar

What would you like a given week to look like when it comes to physical intimacy and sexual behaviors? Would it be like the month you recorded in activity 5? Or would it be different?

Fill in this weekly calendar to show what each of you would like to see in your physical relationship.

	PARTNER 1	PARTNER 2
Sunday		
Monday		
Tuesday		
Wednesday		
Thursday		

	PARTNER 1	PARTNER 2
Friday		
Saturday		

ACTIVITY 7: Sexual Satisfaction

How satisfied are you with your sexual experiences? Take this quiz together to find out.

It's important to be honest but also to consider your partner's feelings and sexual self-esteem. Remember that sex is sometimes about your relationship with yourself.

Answer "true" or "false" for each of the following statements.

1. I feel like I can express my sexual self.

2. I worry about whether I satisfy my partner sexually.

3. I am able to feel sexual pleasure.

4. Sex brings up negative emotions for me.

5. I find my sexual life fulfilling.

6. I feel sexually attractive.

7. Sex often leads me to feeling sexually frustrated.

8. I feel like I have enough sexual expression, either alone or partnered.

9. I have the sex I want.

10. I feel comfortable saying no if I don't want to have sex.

11. I feel unable to express kinks or activities that I'm sexually interested in.

12. I feel like my sex life needs improvement.

RESULTS

Mostly "true," you are very satisfied with your sexuality and your sexual relationship with your partner. You feel comfortable being yourself in the bedroom and are able to set boundaries to have the sex you want.

Mostly "false," something is getting in the way of you having the sex you want or the kind of sexual relationship you want—perhaps past experiences, trauma, or feelings of guilt or shame around your sexuality. It may be helpful for you to see a therapist alone or with your partner.

ACTIVITY 8: Attraction

What do you find attractive about your partner? What about them revs your engine? What do you think most about when you fantasize about your partner? What drew you to them? What keeps you coming back?

Check all the factors of your partner's personality or physical presentation that attract you to them.

PERSONALITY FACTORS

PARTNER 1	PARTNER 2		PARTNER 1	PARTNER 2	
☐	☐	Intelligence	☐	☐	Independence
☐	☐	Generosity	☐	☐	Calmness
☐	☐	Kindness	☐	☐	Confidence
☐	☐	Stability	☐	☐	Charisma
☐	☐	Courage	☐	☐	Reserve
☐	☐	Empathy	☐	☐	Thoughtfulness
☐	☐	Practicality	☐	☐	Goofiness
☐	☐	Adventurousness	☐	☐	Protectiveness
☐	☐	Respectfulness	☐	☐	Happiness
☐	☐	Resilience	☐	☐	Humor
☐	☐	Patience	☐	☐	Cleanliness
☐	☐	Trustworthiness	☐	☐	Passion

☐	☐	Honesty	☐	☐	Wit
☐	☐	Hard work	☐	☐	Other:
☐	☐	Encouragement	☐	☐	Other:
☐	☐	Conversation skills	☐	☐	Other:
☐	☐	Compassion	☐	☐	Other:
☐	☐	Awkwardness	☐	☐	Other:

PHYSICAL FACTORS

PARTNER 1	PARTNER 2		PARTNER 1	PARTNER 2	
☐	☐	Eyes	☐	☐	Fitness
☐	☐	Arms	☐	☐	Teeth
☐	☐	Legs	☐	☐	Jawline
☐	☐	Butt	☐	☐	Bone structure
☐	☐	Chest/Breasts	☐	☐	Style
☐	☐	Muscles	☐	☐	Height
☐	☐	Face	☐	☐	Voice
☐	☐	Smile	☐	☐	Feet
☐	☐	Nose	☐	☐	Smell
☐	☐	Ears	☐	☐	Hands
☐	☐	Piercings	☐	☐	Other:
☐	☐	Tattoos	☐	☐	Other:
☐	☐	Hair color	☐	☐	Other:
☐	☐	Genitals			
☐	☐	Facial hair			
☐	☐	Hairstyle			
☐	☐	Dress			
☐	☐	Body language			
☐	☐	Curves			

There are many different words and categories to describe your sexual orientation, identity, and way of being in relationships with others. Go through this chart together. Are any terms new to you? Do you see any new ways of describing your sexuality?

If you feel a term applies to you, check the box next to it.

Keep in mind that these terms are always shifting and changing, and folks are free to identify any way they wish!

	DESCRIPTION	PARTNER 1	PARTNER 2
Asexual	No sexual attraction toward others.		
Aromantic	No romantic attraction toward others.		
Gray sexual	Rare sexual attraction toward others.		
Gray romantic	Rare romantic attraction toward others.		
Demisexual	Sexual attraction only occurs when there is an emotional connection.		
Demiromantic	Romantic attraction only occurs when there is an emotional connection.		
Heterosexual	Sexual attraction only to those of another gender.		
Heteromantic	Romantic attraction only to those of another gender.		

	DESCRIPTION	PARTNER 1	PARTNER 2
Homosexual	Sexual attraction only to those of the same gender.		
Homoromantic	Romantic attraction only to those of the same gender.		
Bisexual	Sexual attraction to your gender and other genders.		
Biromantic	Romantic attraction to your gender and other genders.		
Pansexual	Sexual attraction occurs regardless of gender identity.		
Panromantic	Romantic attraction occurs regardless of gender identity.		
Polysexual	The ability to experience sexual attraction to more than one person at once.		
Polyromantic	The ability to experience romantic attraction to more than one person at once.		

(This chart is loosely based on the article "What's in a Name? Exploring Use of the Word Queer as a Term of Identification Within the College-Aged LGBT Community" by Diane L. Zosky and Robert Alberts.)

What do you like most about your partner's sexuality? What surprised you about your partner's responses?

Partner 1:

_____

_____

_____

Partner 2:

_____

_____

_____

Do you feel like your and your partner's sexual interests, orientations, libidos, and identities fit well together? Do you feel like you're compatible?

_____

_____

In what areas (if any) do you feel like you and your partner are not compatible?

_____

_____

_____

What sexual compromises can you make?

_____

_____

_____

_____

My work with couples has shown me that, like many other aspects of sexuality, relationship orientation is nonbinary; we all exist on a spectrum of monogamy and non-monogamy. This activity asks where you and your partner each fall on that spectrum.

For each statement, answer "true" or "false."

1. I am capable of having platonic love for more than one person.

2. I am capable of having romantic love for more than one person.

3. I am capable of being sexually attracted to more than one person.

4. I am capable of having emotional relationships with multiple people at once.

5. I am capable of having sexual relationships with multiple people at once.

6. I believe that love is an infinite resource.

7. I am comfortable with my partner having an emotional connection with someone else.

8. I am comfortable with my partner having a physical or sexual connection with someone else.

9. Sex and love are different things to me.

10. I trust my partner to be honest with me.

11. I trust that my partner would be honest with other people.

12. I trust that my partner would communicate about safe sex if they were to have sex with other partners.

13. My partner can go out on their own, and it doesn't cause me any stress.

14. It makes me feel happy when I see my partner happy.

15. I trust the assurance I get from my partner that they love me.

16. I am interested in exploring non-monogamy.

RESULTS

Mostly "true," it may be time for you to consider non-monogamy and see if it feels suited to your relationship. In the next activity, we'll talk about different ways to practice non-monogamy.

Mostly "false," it sounds like monogamy is for you. And there's nothing wrong with that! Monogamy has worked for many over the course of human history.

Mostly disagreed, you and your partner may have different ideas about what your relationship could look like. Keep going through the next few activities and perhaps return to this activity later. If you think this difference in perspective might impact your relationship, it may be time to talk to a professional about your relationship goals.

ACTIVITY 12: Understanding Non-Monogamy

If you or your partner is interested in exploring non-monogamy, here are some key concepts you should know.

	SUMMARY
Ethical Non-Monogamy	Ethical non-monogamy refers to non-monogamous activities that everyone participating knows about and is able to consent to.
Cheating	What we think of as a traditional affair. Cheating can be either physical or emotional, and it is the only form of non-monogamy that is nonconsensual.
Swinging	Swinging usually involves individuals or established couples who come together for a no-strings-attached sexual activity. Some swingers might have romantic or emotional connections with their extramarital sexual partners, but often it's more of an acquaintance or friend-with-benefits-type situation.

	SUMMARY
Monogamish	Monogamish folks are mostly monogamous but open to non-monogamy. Monogamish folks might practice non-monogamy once in the course of their relationship, once a year, or even once a month or more, but they identify as monogamous more often than not.
Open Relationships	Folks in open relationships might have casual sexual encounters; more serious, long-term relationships; or anything in between. Some partners in open relationships agree to a "don't ask, don't tell" policy; others agree to communicate directly about their sexual experiences with others outside their primary relationship.
Polyamory	Polyamory was developed out of the ideology that love, sex, and romance are not meant to be shared with only one person. Polyamorous folks might form a "polycule" or have overlapping sexual or romantic partners with their partners, but not always.
Poly/mono	Poly/mono refers to a partnership where one person chooses monogamy and the other does not. There are many reasons partners might do so. Perhaps the poly person has a sexual need that the mono person isn't able to meet. Perhaps something has gotten in the way of the mono person's ability to be sexual, but they want their partner to continue exploring their sexuality.
Polygamy	Polygamy refers to a mostly historical practice that most often involved a man marrying two or more women. This practice is now illegal in the United States, with some exceptions. Many people confuse polyamory with polygamy, but the two ideologies are very different.
Relationship Anarchy	Relationship anarchy refers to folks who don't agree with the idea of following a relationship hierarchy. Having a "primary partner" or a spouse might be outside the norm for someone who practices relationship anarchy.

ACTIVITY 13: Sexual Boundaries

Let's get a sense of your sexual boundaries. Put an X beside any activity that feels like a definite no for you. Put a check mark if it's something you might want to explore, but you're not sure. Put a star for any in which you are definitely interested or already doing.

PARTNER 1	PARTNER 2	
☐	☐	Your partner views pornography.
☐	☐	Your partner fantasizes about someone else.
☐	☐	Your partner is sexually attracted to a celebrity or public figure.
☐	☐	Your partner fantasizes about a celebrity or public figure.
☐	☐	Your partner is sexually attracted to a person you know.
☐	☐	Your partner fantasizes about a person you know.
☐	☐	Your partner has a crush.
☐	☐	Your partner has an emotional connection with a friend who they're not attracted to.
☐	☐	Your partner has an emotional connection with a friend who they are attracted to.
☐	☐	Your partner holds hands with another person.
☐	☐	Your partner hugs another person.
☐	☐	Your partner hugs a person you suspect they might be attracted to.
☐	☐	Your partner flirts with someone without you there.
☐	☐	Your partner flirts with someone while you're there.
☐	☐	Your partner dances with someone when you're not there.
☐	☐	Your partner dances with someone while you're there.
☐	☐	Your partner kisses another person.
☐	☐	Your partner sends a sexual text to another person.
☐	☐	Your partner confesses their interest in another person.

☐	☐	Your partner spends the night at a friend's house.
☐	☐	Your partner spends the night at a friend's house who you suspect they might be attracted to.
☐	☐	Your partner makes out with someone when you're not there.
☐	☐	Your partner makes out with someone while you're there.
☐	☐	Your partner has sex with someone when you're not there.
☐	☐	Your partner has sex with someone while you're there.

ACTIVITY 14: Exploring Monogamy and Non-Monogamy

What did you learn about monogamy and non-monogamy from activities 11 and 12?

_____

_____

_____

_____

_____

_____

_____

What did you learn about your partner's sexual boundaries in activity 13?

Partner 1:

_____

_____

_____

Partner 2:

_____

_____

_____

_____

What (if anything) would you like to explore about monogamy and non-monogamy in your relationship?

_____

_____

_____

Have any of the activities you've done so far in this chapter brought up any feelings or insecurities about your relationship?

_____

_____

_____

In your relationship, what sexual boundaries are the most important?

_____

_____

_____

In your relationship, do you feel like you have a good idea how to meet these boundaries and expectations? For example, if one of your relationship boundaries is that you are not permitted to flirt with anyone, do you have a good sense of what flirting *means*?

_____

_____

_____

_____

Clarify what boundaries are important to you and specifically what they mean.

_____

_____

_____

_____

_____

ACTIVITY 15: Kink Exploration

Kinky or vanilla—how do you identify? Here's a chart explaining different types of sexual acts. If one interests you, give it a check mark.

TYPE OF SEXUAL BEHAVIOR	SUMMARY	PARTNER 1	PARTNER 2
Vanilla	Vanilla behaviors refers to more "typical" sexual acts, such as common sexual positions (e.g., missionary or doggy style) and common sexual acts (e.g., oral sex and masturbation).		
Impact	Impact play refers to a variety of activities involving spanking or hitting your partner with a hand or a tool.		
Torture	Torture play involves physically hurting or torturing your partner, such as crushing, stretching, or twisting their genitals.		
Domination	Domination involves a power exchange between partners that might include a variety of different activities, including humiliation, teasing, and using control or power for sexual play.		
Restraint	Restraint play involves using handcuffs, rope, ties, locks, or other mechanisms to restrain your partner during sexual play.		
Medical	Medical kinks involve using devices such as enemas, needles, or other medical objects upon your partner.		

TYPE OF SEXUAL BEHAVIOR	SUMMARY	PARTNER 1	PARTNER 2
Role-Play	There are many possible role-play kinks, from teachers and students to doctors and patients, pony play, puppy play, or cross-dressing.		
Sensation Play	This play involves using items to induce different physical sensations, such as hot wax, electricity, or certain types of cupping and massage.		
Butt Stuff	This category encompasses anything from anal sex to rimming, prostate massage, and pegging.		
Materials	Some folks find different materials, such as latex, fur, nylon, or PVC sexy.		
Sexual Acts	You can have a kink around a certain sexual act or experience, like a blowjob, squirting, or even ejaculation.		
Body Paraphilias	A body paraphilia is an attraction to a certain type of body, like an older adult's body, or a body part, like a foot or a breast.		
Object Paraphilias	An object paraphilia is an attraction to a certain object, like a balloon, a car, a tree, or a stuffed animal.		

TYPE OF SEXUAL BEHAVIOR	SUMMARY	PARTNER 1	PARTNER 2
Bodily Function Paraphilias	These paraphilias refer to a sexual interest in certain bodily functions, such as urinating, defecating, spitting, or menstruation.		
Miscellaneous	There are far more types of kinks than can possibly be listed here—from hentai to feeding to fantasies around cannibalism.		

(Some descriptions taken from the "Periodic Table of Kink" by Uberkinky.)

ACTIVITY 16: Fantasy

Do you fantasize about your partner? If yes, what do you fantasize about?

Partner 1:

_____

_____

_____

_____

_____

Partner 2:

_____

_____

_____

_____

_____

Do you ever have sexual dreams about your partner? If so, what was the steamiest one?

Partner 1:

_____

_____

_____

_____

Partner 2:

_____

_____

_____

_____

What's a fantasy involving your partner that you want to explore?

Partner 1:

_____

_____

_____

_____

Partner 2:

_____

_____

_____

_____

The Dual Control Model

The dual control model of sexual response is the new gold standard for understanding human sexuality. This model teaches us that there are two factors that go into whether we're having sex: sexual excitation and sexual inhibition.

Sexual excitation factors act like a gas pedal that makes it more likely that you'll have sex, whereas sexual inhibition factors act like the brakes, decreasing the likelihood of a sexual experience.

A human will only engage in sexual behaviors if the factors of sexual excitation outweigh the factors of sexual inhibition. So the car only gets moving if the gas is working harder than the brakes.

Everyone has a different set of inhibition factors and excitation factors. If you and your partner are hoping to increase your sexual frequency, it's time to learn your partner's gas and brakes.

Here are some examples:

Sexual Inhibitory Factors (Brakes)
- Stress
- Exhaustion
- Trauma
- A lack of trust
- Shame/guilt about sexuality
- An uncomfortable setting

Sexual Excitation Factors (Gas Pedal)
- Fantasizing about your partner
- Being on vacation
- Sexual novelty
- Physical attraction
- Feeling connected to your partner
- Foreplay

ACTIVITY 17: Sexuality Spectrums

Where are you on the spectrums of sexuality? On the following lines, make a vertical line for you and a line for your partner signifying where you feel like you fall on these spectrums. Use a different color pen so you know who's who.

How comfortable do you feel talking to your partner about sex?

Not very comfortable   In the middle   Very comfortable

How much does your sexual script feel predictable and routine?

Not very routine   In the middle   Very routine

How satisfied do you feel with the sex that you're having?

Not very satisfied   In the middle   Very satisfied

How attracted do you feel to your partner?

Not very attracted   In the middle   Very attracted

Do you feel like your and your partner's sexual personalities are compatible?

Not very compatible   In the middle   Very compatible

How strong is your libido, or your desire for sex?

Not very strong   In the middle   Very strong

Where do you feel like you land on the spectrum of monogamy and non-monogamy?

Very non-monogamous   In the middle   Very monogamous

How kinky do you identify as?

Vanilla   In the middle   Very kinky

Are you a fantasizer?

⏺ ·· ⏺

I don't fantasize.　　　　In the middle　　　　I fantasize often.

How do you identify your sexual orientation?

⏺ ·· ⏺

Heterosexual　　　　Bisexual/pansexual　　　　Homosexual

or something else: _____

How do you identify your gender?

⏺ ·· ⏺

Cisgender　　　　Nonbinary　　　　Transgender

or something else: _____

How do you identify your interest in sex?

⏺ ·· ⏺

Ace/asexual　　　　Demisexual　　　　Hypersexual

How surprised were you by your partner's answers in this section?

⏺ ·· ⏺

Not surprised　　　　In the middle　　　　Very surprised

ACTIVITY 18: End-of-Chapter Check-In

What did you learn about your own or your partner's sexuality?

Partner 1:

_____

_____

_____

Partner 2:

_____

_____

_____

Do you think your partner is the same person sexually that they were when you first met them? What about when you were first married or first in a relationship?

Partner 1:

_____

_____

_____

Partner 2:

_____

_____

_____

Do you think your partner is the same sexual person today as they were to you yesterday? What do you think this chapter's activities have done to deepen your sexual relationship with your partner?

Partner 1:

_____

_____

_____

Partner 2:

_____

_____

_____

Physical Intimacy and Sexuality: Five Takeaways

1. **Sexual evolution.** Sexuality isn't something we're ever done exploring with our partner. There are peaks and valleys in every sexual relationship.

2. **Monogamy and non-monogamy**. No single relationship orientation is for everyone. Setting boundaries and expectations clearly and directly is the best way to avoid a relationship style that doesn't work for both monogamous and non-monogamous folks.

3. **Kinky can be fun.** There's no right way to have sex, but exploring kinks can be super fun.

4. **Identity on your own terms.** There are many different words and categories to describe your sexual orientation, identity, and way of being in relationships with others. But these terms are always shifting and changing, and you're always free to identify any way you wish!

5. **Spectrums of sexuality.** As a partner, it is your job to love and respect your partner regardless of how they identify. Love is love!

Physical Intimacy and Sexuality: Five Conflict-Management Strategies

1. **Explore your sexual scripts.** For some, a sexual routine is helpful in maintaining your sexual relationship. For others, it's a barrier. Check in with your partner about what they need to make sex awesome!

2. **Share your attraction.** Tell your partner what you find attractive about them. Regular reminders will increase the satisfaction in your relationship, both sexually and emotionally.

3. **Talk about your insecurities.** When you're feeling insecure about your body, your sexuality, or your sexual relationship, put those feelings out on the table and work on them together.

4. **Think ahead.** What do you and your partner plan to do if one of you crosses a sexual boundary the other has set?

5. **Meet what needs you can.** Remember that it's not your job to meet every one of your partner's needs.

CHAPTER 6

Family, Friends, and Communication

Aside from our partner, our family and friends are often the people we choose to spend the most time with.

"Family" means different things to different people; not all families are biological or folks we're set up with in childhood. Changes in the ways we live, with whom we live, and what our communities look like mean that many folks today place meaning on chosen family, the people we choose to have in our lives if our family of origin is not a part of our lives.

In this chapter, you will find activities that explore your family story as well as uncover your and your partner's mutual desired experience of family. For all these activities, feel free to think about your chosen family instead of your traditional family if your family of origin is not meaningful to you for whatever reason.

Our friendships might be equally as important! Friends can even be our chosen family. Not only are our friendships valuable to us personally, but they impact our partnerships, so we'll be exploring your ideas about friends and friendship in this chapter as well.

Finally, we'll come back to a couple of topics from the beginning of the book, listening and conflict management, with some activities that allow you to practice the skills you learned in part 1.

ACTIVITY 1: Family Feelings

When you think about family, what emotions come up for you? Do you feel warm and fuzzy feelings? Or are things more complicated?

Use this checklist to identify your feelings about the idea of family. Put a check mark next to the feelings or attributes that match your experience of family.

PARTNER 1	PARTNER 2		PARTNER 1	PARTNER 2	
☐	☐	Comforted	☐	☐	Stressed
☐	☐	Warm	☐	☐	Grateful
☐	☐	Cared for	☐	☐	Burdened
☐	☐	Playful	☐	☐	Hopeless
☐	☐	Insulted	☐	☐	Remorseful
☐	☐	Lonely	☐	☐	Adored
☐	☐	Traumatic	☐	☐	Excited
☐	☐	Discouraged	☐	☐	Appreciated
☐	☐	Spiteful	☐	☐	Defensive
☐	☐	Gloomy	☐	☐	Hostile
☐	☐	Silly	☐	☐	Vengeful
☐	☐	Humorous	☐	☐	Frustrated
☐	☐	Cold	☐	☐	Violated
☐	☐	Angry	☐	☐	Pestered
☐	☐	Supported	☐	☐	Cantankerous
☐	☐	Wild	☐	☐	Let down
☐	☐	Annoyed	☐	☐	Responsible
☐	☐	Gregarious	☐	☐	Cautious
☐	☐	Bitter	☐	☐	Anxious
☐	☐	Uplifted	☐	☐	Sick
☐	☐	Neglectful	☐	☐	Uncomfortable
☐	☐	Energetic	☐	☐	Incompatible
☐	☐	Chaotic	☐	☐	Other:
☐	☐	Friendly	☐	☐	Other:
☐	☐	Loud	☐	☐	Other:
☐	☐	Quiet	☐	☐	Other:
☐	☐	Joyful	☐	☐	Other:
☐	☐	Fearful	☐	☐	Other:
☐	☐	Unhappy	☐	☐	Other:

Your upbringing sets the stage for your family values. Even if family is just you and your partner, your definition of family is important to explore.

For each statement, answer "true" or "false."

1. When I was growing up, I generally liked spending time with my family.

2. My family pushed me to be successful in what was important to me.

3. My family had shared interests, hobbies, or beliefs.

4. I felt like my family cared about my feelings.

5. For the most part, I admire my family members.

6. I feel grateful for my family's support.

7. I feel like I could count on my family if I was in a bind.

8. My family expressed positive feelings or pride toward me.

9. I had some control over my choices in my family of origin.

10. My family did their best to provide help when I needed it.

11. If my family had a conflict, we worked through it.

12. My concerns were not ignored or avoided in my family.

13. I saw others safely express emotions in my family.

14. My family modeled appropriate behavior for me.

15. I feel like most members of my family manage their own emotions.

16. I have positive memories from my childhood.

17. It was okay for my family to disagree around opinions or beliefs.

RESULTS

Mostly "true," you have feelings of being supported and respected in your family of origin. The idea of family may feel safe to you!

Mostly "false," you may have had a more challenging upbringing, with aspects that were hard for you to navigate. You may feel anxious in relationships, or perhaps have done some great work to heal.

Adverse Childhood Experiences (ACE) Study

In the mid-1990s, the US Centers for Disease Control and Prevention (CDC) and Kaiser Permanente conducted a study to see the impact of childhood experiences on health and wellness outcomes. Called the ACE Study, it was largest study of its time on this topic.

The study found that health and wellness outcomes were affected by these factors in people's upbringings: physical, emotional, and sexual abuse; violence; substance abuse; mental illness; incarceration; parental separation/divorce; and emotional and physical neglect.

If someone experienced those factors in childhood, they were more likely to experience the following as an adult:

» Injury (such as traumatic brain injury and broken bones)
» Mental illnesses (like depression, anxiety, and post-traumatic stress)
» Reduced maternal health (such as unplanned pregnancy, complications in pregnancy and birth, and fetal death)
» Infectious diseases (including HIV and other STIs)
» Chronic diseases (such as cancer and diabetes)
» Risky behaviors (such as alcohol or drug abuse and unsafe sex)
» Lower levels of education and career exploration
» Lower-than-average income

In the original study, about 36.1 percent of respondents had zero ACE factors, 26 percent had one, 15.9 percent had two, 9.5 percent had three, and 12.5 percent had four or more factors. Findings show that the risk for negative outcomes increases with each ACE factor a person has.

It's likely that the overall prevalence of ACE factors is higher than this study showed. The study's participants were all part of a highly privileged population. They resided in Southern California, had insurance coverage, and were largely white folks with a college degree or other higher education.

Your own ACEs certainly set the tone for what your marriage and lifestyle might look like.

ACTIVITY 3: **Adverse Childhood Experiences Scale**

This activity evaluates adverse childhood experiences (ACEs) and the effects they may have on your mental and physical health. Check the things you experienced prior to age 18. At the end, count up the number of checks to see your ACEs score.

PARTNER 1   PARTNER 2

☐	☐	Did a parent or other adult in your household often swear at you, put you down, humiliate you, or act in a way that made you afraid that you might be physically hurt?
☐	☐	Did a parent or other adult in your household often push you, grab you, slap you, throw things at you, hurt you in a way that left marks or caused you to be injured, or otherwise physically threaten you?
☐	☐	Did an adult person at least five years older than you ever touch you in a sexual way; have you touch their body in a sexual way; try to have oral, anal, or vaginal sex with you; or ask you to engage in other sexual behaviors?
☐	☐	Did you often feel that no one in your family loved you or thought you were important or special? Or did you often feel that your family didn't look out for one another, feel close to one another, or support one another?
☐	☐	Did you often feel that you didn't have enough to eat, had to wear dirty clothes, or had no one to protect you? Or that your parents were too drunk or high to take care of you or take you to the doctor if you needed it?
☐	☐	Were your parents separated or divorced?
☐	☐	Was a parent in your home often on the receiving end of physical violence (such as pushing, slapping, biting, having things thrown at them, punching, or beating) or otherwise physically threatened in front of you?
☐	☐	Did you live with anyone who was a problem drinker, alcoholic, or drug user?
☐	☐	Was a household member depressed or mentally ill? Or did a household member attempt suicide or engage in self-harming behaviors?
☐	☐	Did a household member go to prison?
_____	_____	TOTAL ACEs SCORES

ACTIVITY 4: Family History

How much do you know about where you come from? This checklist is a great way to identify things you know or don't know about your family and what you'd like to find out more about. These topics are great questions for your eldest family members, if you have access to them. If you have an opportunity to be with your family, bring this list along and see if you get any interesting conversations out of it.

To some extent, your partner's family is also your family. This checklist will also help you learn more about your partner's family history.

Put a check mark beside a statement if it's information you think you already know about your family. Put an X if you don't know yet. Share the information you know with your partner.

PARTNER 1	PARTNER 2	
☐	☐	The names of everyone in your family all the way up to your great-grandparents
☐	☐	Names of family members beyond your great-grandparents
☐	☐	General birth dates and birthplaces of your extended family
☐	☐	Occupations of your family members
☐	☐	Immigration patterns
☐	☐	Cultural rituals from your family of origin
☐	☐	Important foods from your family of origin
☐	☐	Languages spoken by your family of origin
☐	☐	A story or personality factor about most family members
☐	☐	Major family secrets
☐	☐	A family joke
☐	☐	Your family's biggest challenge
☐	☐	Your family's greatest accomplishment
☐	☐	Patterns of spiritual or religious beliefs in your family
☐	☐	Resting places for important family members
☐	☐	A memorable moment in your family's history
☐	☐	Your coolest family member
☐	☐	The oldest living person in your family tree
☐	☐	A love story in your family

☐	☐	Career or education patterns in your family
☐	☐	Interests or hobby patterns in your extended family
☐	☐	Health patterns in your extended family
☐	☐	Substance use patterns in your extended family
☐	☐	Trauma in your extended family

ACTIVITY 5: Your Family Tree

In this activity, you'll put together a family tree, or "genogram" in clinical terms.

First, put together what you know about your family from the previous exercise, writing down all of their names on a separate piece of paper in a family tree format. Then grab some colored pencils, pens, or crayons.

Think about what relationships are conflicted or challenging and draw an angry little red wavy line in between people who don't get along.

Next, think about who's the closest to each other. Draw a green line between people who are closer than close.

What patterns do you see? Think about what you discussed in activity 4 and build on it.

Are there any family patterns in religion, beliefs, lifestyle, political affiliation, being emotionally cut off, physical illness, trauma, immigration, child rearing, education, occupation, finances, artistic ability, cultures, ethnicities, personalities, or levels of privilege? Any differences in these factors? Anything else you can think of?

Keep your family tree handy. You'll be using it in activity 6.

ACTIVITY 6: What Do You Know about Your Family Histories?

Let's assess what you and your partner learned about yourself and each other in activity 5—and how this information will help you communicate more effectively.

Did activity 5 cause you to think any differently about your family? Any surprises or things you didn't notice before?

Partner 1:

_____

_____

_____

Partner 2:

_____

_____

_____

What about your partner's family? What did you learn that you didn't already know?

Partner 1:

_____

_____

_____

Partner 2:

_____

_____

_____

What patterns did you notice in each of your family trees? Were there any patterns that were present in both of your families?

Partner 1:

_____

_____

_____

Partner 2:

_____

_____

_____

Are the patterns in each of your families talked about openly? Or are they more along the line of family secrets? Do family members communicate about family issues?

Partner 1:

_____

_____

_____

Partner 2:

_____

_____

_____

What strengths are present in each of your families? What weaknesses?
Partner 1:

_____

_____

Partner 2:

_____

_____

What spoken or unspoken rules do you see in these patterns? Are family members allowed to break from the norm? Or are differences not welcomed?
Partner 1:

_____

_____

Partner 2:

_____

_____

How do these ideas impact you and your partner's relationship and immediate family system?
Partner 1:

_____

_____

Partner 2:

_____

_____

ACTIVITY 7: Holiday Planning

The cultural traditions present in both of your families are sure to be different, and these differences can bring up conflict in relationships. What do holidays look like in your family? How do you celebrate them? Are there any rituals, celebrations, or traditions that are important to you and your families?

Draw up a calendar of important holidays and think about how they are celebrated in each other's family. You can use something like the calendar below.

DAY	PARTNER 1	PARTNER 2

ACTIVITY 8: Family Values

We've talked about patterns in your family of origin and your childhood. What family values are most important to you as you manifest your own family (whatever family might mean to you)?

Choose 15 of the following values that are most important to you. Which are your top five? What was on your list? What didn't make the cut?

PARTNER 1	PARTNER 2		PARTNER 1	PARTNER 2	
☐	☐	Hard work	☐	☐	Gratitude
☐	☐	Compassion	☐	☐	Acceptance
☐	☐	Kindness	☐	☐	Cooperation
☐	☐	Creativity	☐	☐	Honesty
☐	☐	Peace	☐	☐	Perseverance
☐	☐	Faith	☐	☐	Trust
☐	☐	Justice	☐	☐	Safety
☐	☐	Equality	☐	☐	Hard work
☐	☐	Generosity	☐	☐	Compromise
☐	☐	Courage	☐	☐	Other:
☐	☐	Integrity	☐	☐	Other:
☐	☐	Respect	☐	☐	Other:
☐	☐	Manners	☐	☐	Other:
☐	☐	Self-control	☐	☐	Other:

ACTIVITY 9: What Does Family Mean to You?

Let's dive deeper into what you're hoping to create in your own family. Many disagreements come when we don't know what our shared goals are. Clarifying values can help you feel more on the same page.

Do you and your partner share the same family values?

_____

_____

What did each of you rank as your top five family values that you hope to manifest in your household?

Partner 1:

_____

_____

Partner 2:

_____

_____

Were your top five values the same or different?

_____

_____

_____

What do you think inspired the values that are most important to you?

Partner 1:

_____

_____

_____

Partner 2:

_____

_____

_____

What do you think made you and your partner choose different values? Upbringing? Childhood experiences? Culture? Religion?

Partner 1:

_____

_____

_____

Partner 2:

_____

_____

_____

Do any of these value differences pose a challenge in your relationship? How so? If they do, how will you compromise or negotiate around these differences in values?

_____

_____

_____

ACTIVITY 10: **The Future of Your Family**

If you don't discuss your individual goals with your partner, you might not realize that the two of you are working toward completely different goals.

This quiz will help you identify things you and your partner might need or want to discuss regarding your family's future. Feel free to start with the goals you and your partner identified and discussed in the chapter 2 activities.

Write yes or no next to each goal or question.
Do you hope to:

PARTNER 1   PARTNER 2

_____   _____   **Live in a different city**

Have you thought about what your plans might be?

Have you discussed this with your partner?

Have you and your partner made plans to make this happen?

Are you close to making this goal happen?

_____   _____   **Live in a different home nearby**

Have you thought about what your plans might be?

Have you discussed this with your partner?

Have you and your partner made plans to make this happen?

Are you close to making this goal happen?

_____   _____   **Make a large purchase (such as a home, boat, RV, vehicle, or vacation)**

_____   _____   Have you thought about what your plans might be?

_____   _____   Have you discussed this with your partner?

_____   _____   Have you and your partner made plans to make this happen?

_____   _____   Are you close to making this goal happen?

_____   _____   **Get a pet**

_____   _____   Have you thought about what your plans might be?

_____   _____   Have you discussed this with your partner?

_____   _____   Have you and your partner made plans to make this happen?

_____   _____   Are you close to making this goal happen?

_____   _____   **Adopt/foster/have a child**

_____   _____   Have you thought about what your plans might be?

_____   _____   Have you discussed this with your partner?

_____   _____   Have you and your partner made plans to make this happen?

_____   _____   Are you close to making this goal happen?

_____   _____   **Other:** _____

_____   _____   Have you thought about what your plans might be?

_____   _____   Have you discussed this with your partner?

_____   _____   Have you and your partner made plans to make this happen?

_____   _____   Are you close to making this goal happen?

_____   _____   **Other:** _____

_____   Have you thought about what your plans might be?

_____   Have you discussed this with your partner?

_____   Have you and your partner made plans to make
                    this happen?

_____   Are you close to making this goal happen?

ACTIVITY 11: Expanding Your Family

This chart lists some common family planning topics. Use this as a way to talk
about future parenting or caregiving goals, whatever that might mean to you.
Put a check mark in the columns on the right if you want to talk about the topic
or if it's something you've talked about or resolved. Focus on the topics that are
applicable to you.

TOPIC	EXPLANATION	I WANT TO TALK ABOUT IT.	WE'VE TALKED ABOUT IT OR RESOLVED IT.
Contraception	How might you prevent an unplanned pregnancy?		
Being a Parent	Do you both want to be a parent?		
Fertility	Do you want biological children? Have either of you investigated your fertility?		
Infertility	What would it mean if you were unable to have a biological child for whatever reason?		
Surrogacy	What are your feelings on using a surrogate as a way of being a parent?		

TOPIC	EXPLANATION	I WANT TO TALK ABOUT IT.	WE'VE TALKED ABOUT IT OR RESOLVED IT.
Foster Care	What are your feelings on foster care as a way of being a parent?		
Adoption	What are your feelings on adoption as a way of being a parent?		
Growing a Family	If you and your partner already have a child or children, are you hoping to expand your family? How large of a family might you want?		
Blending a Family	Do you and your partner have children from other partnerships? How do you want to blend these families? What are your goals for an already blended family? How do you hope to increase feelings of closeness or harmony in this family system?		
Pet Parenting	Are you and your partner hoping to expand your family with any nonhuman animals?		
Caregiving for a Friend or Family Member	Do you and your partner have plans to take care of a family member as they age? What about a friend or relative if they were to become ill?		

ACTIVITY 12: How Do You Want to Parent?

This is a continuation of the previous activity. If you and your partner have a child or are hoping to be parents, here are some conversations that may be important to have. Some of these questions might be relevant for those hoping to add pets to the family as well!

TOPIC	EXPLANATION	IT'S SOMETHING WE'VE HAD CONVERSATIONS ABOUT.	IT'S SOMETHING WE'VE RESOLVED.
Childcare	Would there be a primary caregiver for the child? Would one partner stay home? Would responsibilities be split evenly?		
Discipline	How would you want to discipline your child? What would consequences be for inappropriate behaviors? What models of parenting are you interested in?		
Change	How prepared are you that your relationship could change? What ways are you "okay" with your relationship changing? What things do you strongly feel that you do not want to change?		
Couple Strength	How strong do you feel as a couple? How might you resolve problems or challenges that might come up as you are parenting? Do you and your partner feel like a team?		

TOPIC	EXPLANATION	IT'S SOMETHING WE'VE HAD CONVERSATIONS ABOUT.	IT'S SOMETHING WE'VE RESOLVED.
Values	What beliefs, values, and spiritual or religious ideals are important for you to pass on to your family?		
Timing	How will you know that it's the right time for a new child? How will you decide?		
Change of Heart	What if one partner were to change their mind about having children? What would that mean for the partnership?		
Lifestyle Choices	Will you feed the child breast milk or formula? Will you vaccinate? Will you co-sleep with your child? What would be your birth plan? How much screen time would your child be allowed? Will you save for their education? Who will go back to work after baby and when? How would you want your child to be educated? What if one of you needs a break? Anything else you can think of?		

ACTIVITY 13: What's the Meaning of Friendship?

After your partner (and maybe your family or your coworkers), your friends are the next biggest social commitment in your lives. Do you and your partner feel the same way about friendships? Do you seek the same things from your friends? Let's find out.

Check five items from the following list that you consider *musts* in your friendships.

PARTNER 1 PARTNER 2

PARTNER 1	PARTNER 2	
☐	☐	Mutual hobbies or shared interests
☐	☐	Regular communication
☐	☐	Emotional intimacy
☐	☐	Playing sports together
☐	☐	Physical intimacy
☐	☐	Convenience
☐	☐	Independence
☐	☐	Support or validation
☐	☐	Companionship
☐	☐	Trust
☐	☐	Shared values
☐	☐	A sense of humor
☐	☐	A positive attitude
☐	☐	Vulnerability
☐	☐	Shared religious or spiritual beliefs
☐	☐	Cynicism, sarcasm, or wit
☐	☐	Respect
☐	☐	Love
☐	☐	Initiation of social contact
☐	☐	Shows interest in you/your life
☐	☐	Gives gifts
☐	☐	Commitment (like best friendship)
☐	☐	Giving advice

☐	☐	Compatibility
☐	☐	Playfulness
☐	☐	Gives you space
☐	☐	Length or duration of friendship
☐	☐	Loyalty
☐	☐	Safety
☐	☐	Teases you/jokes with you
☐	☐	Adventurousness
☐	☐	Other:
☐	☐	Other:
☐	☐	Other:

Compare each other's top five items. Did you select similar musts? Were you surprised by what your partner selected? Are there other important features you did not include in your top five items that are still of value to you? What are they?

ACTIVITY 14: Social Schedule

Let's think about how your social activities affect your marriage. Use this tool to plan your next week of social engagements. As you do, think about the following: How do you and your partner balance time together with social time? Who's more social? Who's more of a homebody? Do you and your partner ever have conflict when it comes to managing your social schedule? If so, what sorts of challenges come up? Do you want more time or less time together?

	PARTNER 1	PARTNER 2
Sunday		
Monday		

	PARTNER 1	PARTNER 2
Tuesday		
Wednesday		
Thursday		
Friday		
Saturday		

ACTIVITY 15: Who Are Your Friends?

You should know who the important players are in your partner's life. But do you? Let's find out!

You'll need two sheets of paper for this exercise, one for each partner. Read each question out loud. Then, on your sheet of paper, write down the question number and how you think *your partner* would answer the question.

After you've gone through all the questions, swap papers and review each other's guesses. Circle the answers your partner got right. Next to any incorrect guesses, write your actual answer.

1. Who is your partner's oldest friend from childhood?

2. Who is your partner's newest friend?

3. Who is your partner's best friend?

4. Who would your partner trust with a big secret?

5. Who is your partner most likely to do something wild with?

6. Besides you, whom would your partner call if there were an emergency?

7. Who is their closest family friend?

8. Who is someone your partner didn't like at first but now is someone they love?

9. Who's a formerly close friend of your partner's?

10. Who's someone your partner wishes were a closer friend?

11. Who is your partner most likely to be texting regularly?

ACTIVITY 16: Being a Good Listener

Now let's return to an important topic from the beginning of this book: listening.

What does it mean to be a good listener? In chapter 1, we talked about some of the skills that go into active listening. Let's quickly review those skills again in preparation for activity 17.

SKILL	EXPLANATION
Eye Contact	Make direct eye contact with your partner to show that your focus and attention are on them.
Facing Your Partner	Direct your body toward your partner as they speak.
Showing Interest	Nod and communicate that you're following along by using "mmm," "I see," or other verbal signs of interest.
Focus	Sit still, not looking at your phone or the TV or being distracted by the environment.

SKILL	EXPLANATION
Pausing	Wait for your partner to complete a thought before interjecting or adding opinions or thoughts to the conversation.
Reflecting	Repeat or paraphrase what your partner has said.
Asking for Clarity	Make sure you understand your partner's feelings. Ask, "Did I get that right?" after you summarize what you heard.
Open-Ended Questions	Ask questions about the situation, more complex than simple yes/no questions.
Validating	Identify or predict how your partner might be feeling. Normalize your partner's experience and emotions. Provide support, encouragement, or feedback around their experience. Speak from your heart about how their story makes you feel.

ACTIVITY 17: Practice Validation and Active Listening

This activity gives you the opportunity to practice the listening skills from activity 16. You'll go through this activity twice so each of you can take a turn being the sharer and the listener.

First, partner 1 will choose a topic and share their thoughts, feelings, and opinions about it. Partner 2 will listen, applying listening skills from activity 16 as they do.

Then you'll switch roles. Partner 2 can introduce a new topic or share what they think or how they feel about the previous topic. Partner 1 will listen, practice listening skills from activity 16 as they do.

After each of you has had a chance to talk and to listen, answer the following questions.

What skills did you notice were the most meaningful to you?

Partner 1:

_____

Partner 2:

_____

Which skills seemed to impact the conversation the least?

Partner 1:

_____

Partner 2:

_____

Which skills would you like your partner to work on?

Partner 1:

_____

Partner 2:

_____

Which skills do you want to work on?

Partner 1:

_____

Partner 2:

_____

ACTIVITY 18: What's Your Conflict Temperature?

When I talk about temperature in conflict, I mean the amount of "heatedness," passion, upset, or distress you feel during a conflict. This quiz will help you understand where you fall on the conflict temperature spectrum. Where you and your partner fall on this spectrum will help you understand how each of you responds to stress or conflict.

Think about a typical conflict in your relationship or a fight or argument you may have been a part of or witnessed. How do you typically respond? Try to focus more on the general patterns you experience in conflict.

Check the items that apply to you.

When I am in conflict, physically, I usually feel:

PARTNER 1	PARTNER 2	
☐	☐	Like my muscles are tense
☐	☐	Like I can't breathe
☐	☐	Shaky
☐	☐	Dizzy or light-headed
☐	☐	Like I have a headache
☐	☐	Like I have a stomachache
☐	☐	A rapid or irregular heartbeat
☐	☐	Sweaty
☐	☐	Like my body feels hot or cold
☐	☐	Like I'm clenching my jaw

When I am in conflict, emotionally, I usually feel:

PARTNER 1	PARTNER 2	
☐	☐	Angry
☐	☐	Resentful
☐	☐	Anxious or worried
☐	☐	Contempt
☐	☐	Overwhelmed with emotion
☐	☐	Vindictive or vengeful
☐	☐	Hurt or sad
☐	☐	Like running away
☐	☐	Shut down, numb, or checked out
☐	☐	Scared or fearful

When I am in conflict, I usually:

☐	☐	Say something hurtful
☐	☐	Swear or curse
☐	☐	Name-call
☐	☐	Cry
☐	☐	Yell
☐	☐	Have a panic attack
☐	☐	Experience racing thoughts
☐	☐	Throw something
☐	☐	Make threats
☐	☐	Leave the area
☐	☐	Other:

RESULTS

The more responses you checked, the more emotionally intense conflict situations might feel for you.

Some of these responses might seem obvious. Of course someone who is screaming and throwing things is upset! But even responses like shutting down, feeling numb, or needing to leave an argument are signs of emotional distress. These responses are examples of what psychologists refer to as emotional flooding.

ACTIVITY 19: Conflict

Building on activity 18, I wonder what conflict patterns you might have come out of your childhood with. Will they be different or the same as your partner's? How might these similarities and differences lead to conflict?

Think about family members who you grew up with. If they did activity 18, would they check more, fewer, or a similar number of statements? Any patterns there?
Partner 1:

_____

_____

_____

Partner 2:

_____

_____

_____

Our conflict temperature may be influenced by our family of origin, our close relationships, or even former partners. Do you see any of these influences in your conflict temperature?

Partner 1:

_____

_____

Partner 2:

_____

_____

Are there any specific fights, situations, or triggers that might elicit higher-temperature responses in you or your partner? What are they?

Partner 1:

_____

_____

Partner 2:

_____

_____

_____

Think about the worst fight you and your partner have had. What made it the worst? Were any of the triggers you identified in activity 18 present?

Partner 1:

_____

_____

_____

Partner 2:

_____

_____

_____

The next time you face a trigger during a conflict, what can you do to prevent the conflict from becoming another "worst" fight?

Partner 1:

_____

_____

_____

Partner 2:

_____

_____

_____

Are you willing to make any promises to your partner to prevent future fights from getting to that level? If so, what are those promises?

_____

_____

_____

Do you and your partner have any goals for conflict?

Partner 1:

_____

_____

_____

Partner 2:

_____

_____

_____

High-Conflict Couples

Psychologists consider "high-conflict couples" to be partners who struggle to regulate their emotions. They often feel high levels of distress during conflict, which often makes their emotions feel out of control.

These couples may display anger, sadness, anxiety, or other high-level distress signals during an argument. High-conflict partners may be more sensitive or reactive to perceived threats, criticism, or emotions of others. They may have a hard time calming down, have fights that last a long time, and experience immense physiological arousal during these fights.

High-conflict couples do not enjoy experiencing conflict-triggered emotional stress. Often, this emotional response is related to their family history and childhood experiences. It can be related to trauma, mental illness, a personality disorder, stress, environmental factors, or many other factors.

If you think that you or your partner might struggle with emotional dysregulation while in conflict, the best thing you can do for your relationship is to seek individual counseling to learn healthy coping skills. Over time, you can transition into couples therapy.

ACTIVITY 20: End-of-Chapter/End-of-Book Check-In

What topics came up from the previous few activities about caregiving and parenting? Are there a lot of conversations that you and your partner need to have? Or do you feel like you're on the same page?

_____

_____

_____

How close do you think you are to reaching resolutions around family planning?

_____

_____

_____

If you're not planning on having children, do you and you partner share similar reasons for not wanting to have children? Do you hope to add pets to your family?

_____

_____

_____

It's been a long ride, but here we are at the end of the book. How do you feel about your progress? What has been the most helpful?

Partner 1:

_____

_____

Partner 2:

_____

_____

What did you learn about your partner from this book? Do you feel like your communication is better or worse after going through this book?

Partner 1:

_____

_____

_____

Partner 2:

_____

_____

_____

What are the biggest things you've grown to respect or appreciate about your partner as a result of going through this workbook together?

Partner 1:

_____

_____

_____

Partner 2:

_____

_____

_____

What's something you've felt proud of yourself for while working through this guide?

Partner 1:

_____

_____

_____

Partner 2:

_____

_____

_____

Family, Friends, and Communication: Five Takeaways

1. **Family history.** There's no way around it: Our childhood affects who we are today. Patterns from our past certainly come out in our relationship and communication.

2. **Parenting.** If you choose to be parents or caregivers of any kind, it's important for you and your partner to discuss your expectations and goals for this aspect of your life together.

3. **Friendships.** Friendships can be just as important as family. It's important for both of you to know who are the most important people in your partner's life outside your relationship.

4. **Safety.** As we learned from the ACE study, feeling physically and emotionally safe is a crucial part of being in a healthy family. It's important to think about how safety may be a contributing factor to communication challenges today.

5. **Communication.** The practice you did in listening is something you can always return to. Feel free to use this activity again if you notice that you and your partner are having trouble in future conflicts.

1. **Legacy.** What impact did your family of origin have on you? Take time to share stories and history with your partner so they can understand why you and your family might behave the way you do. This can prevent conflict before it even starts!

2. **Be aware of trauma triggers.** Pay attention to your trauma triggers and make sure that challenges in communication are about the present and not the past.

3. **Caregiving challenges.** Planning for your current or future family isn't going to prevent the challenges or conflicts you'll face as caregivers, but it sure will help.

4. **Regulate.** Conflict can cause us to feel dysregulated, unsafe, or even flooded. Take time to ground yourself, calm down, cope, and engage in regular self-care to avoid feeling emotionally overwhelmed when you and your partner are in conflict.

5. **Friendships.** You may be surprised by how much your friendships can affect the quality of your romantic relationship. Spending time away from your partner or getting emotional needs met outside your relationship is a good way to prevent or cool off heated interactions.

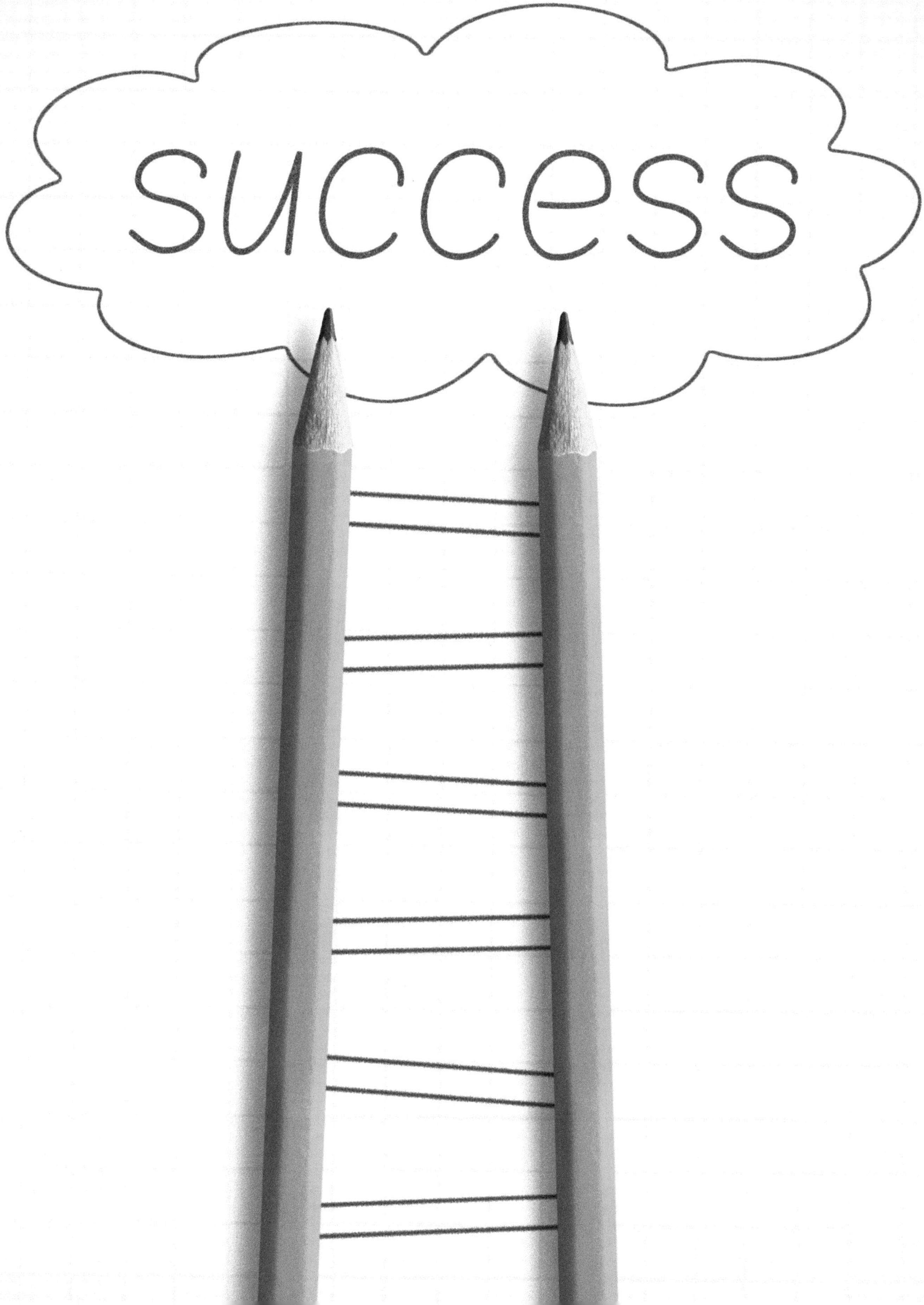
success

A Final Word

My goal with this book was to help you and your partner connect and communicate about topics that we don't always naturally get to chat about. I also wanted to give you opportunities to learn more about each other and what makes each of you tick and to deepen the bond that brought you together in the first place. Did I meet that goal? I sure hope I did.

I hope that you and your partner have found yourselves feeling closer, more understanding of each other, and more appreciative of the love that you've found in this strange little world of ours.

Remember that your relationship is precious, unique, and powerful. While lust, love, and charm connect us, it's communication that keeps us together. Communication is the heart of marriage.

I'll leave you with a quote from one of the great romantics, Carl Sagan: "Every one of us is, in the cosmic perspective, precious. In a hundred billion galaxies, you will not find another."

Resources

Books

Attached: The New Science of Adult Attachment and How It Can Help You Find and Keep Love by Amir Levine and Rachel S. F. Heller

Becoming Attached: First Relationships and How They Shape Our Capacity to Love by Robert Karen

Come as You Are: The Surprising Science That Will Transform Your Sex Life by Emily Nagoski

The Ethical Slut: A Practical Guide to Polyamory, Open Relationships, and Other Freedoms in Sex and Love by Janet W. Hardy and Dossie Easton

The Five Love Languages: The Secret to Love That Lasts by Gary Chapman

The High-Conflict Couple: Dialectical Behavior Therapy Guide to Finding Peace, Intimacy, and Validation by Alan E. Fruzzetti

More Than Two: A Practical Guide To Ethical Polyamory by Franklin Veaux and Eve Rickert

Opening Up: A Guide to Creating and Sustaining Open Relationships by Tristan Taormino

A Secure Base: Parent-Child Attachment and Healthy Human Development by John Bowlby

The Seven Principles for Making Marriage Work: A Practical Guide from the Country's Foremost Relationship Expert by John Gottman and Nan Silver

Online Resources

Adverse childhood experiences: ACEsConnection.com, ACEsTooHigh.com

Attachment quiz: AttachedTheBook.com

Domestic abuse intervention programs: TheDuluthModel.org

Domestic violence resource: LoveIsRespect.org

Ethical non-monogamy: MoreThanTwo.com

The 5 Love Languages: 5LoveLanguages.com

The Gottman Institute: Gottman.com

Health statistics: cdc.gov/sexualhealth/data.html

Sexuality inventory: Mojoupgrade.com

References

Bakermans-Kranenburg, Marian J., and Marinus H. van IJzendoorn. "The First 10,000 Adult Attachment Interviews: Distributions of Adult Attachment Representations in Clinical and Non-Clinical Groups." *Attachment & Human Development* 11, no. 3 (2009): 223–63. doi.org/10.1080/14616730902814762.

Bancroft, John, et al. "The Dual Control Model: Current Status and Future Directions." *Journal of Sex Research* 46, no. 2–3 (2009): 121–42. doi.org/10.1080/00224490902747222.

Bartley, Sharon, Priscilla Blanton, and Jennifer Gilliard. "Husbands and Wives in Dual-Earner Marriages: Decision-Making, Gender Role Attitudes, Division of Household Labor, and Equity." *Marriage and Family Review* 37 (2005): 69–94. doi.org/10.1300/J002v37n04_05.

Baumrind, Diana. "Child Care Practices Anteceding Three Patterns of Preschool Behavior." *Genetic Psychology Monographs 75*, no. 1 (1967): 43–88.

Borreson, Kelly. "These Are the 11 Sex Personality Types, According to a Sex Therapist." *HuffPost*. November 7, 2019. huffpost.com/entry/11-sex-personality-types_l_5dc1c4afe4b0f5dcf8fc375a.

Bowlby, John. *A Secure Base: Parent-Child Attachment and Healthy Human Development.* New York: Basic Books, 1990.

Buettner, Dan. *The Blue Zones: Lessons for Living Longer from the People Who've Lived the Longest*. Washington, DC: National Geographic Society, 2010.

Centers for Disease Control and Prevention. "About the CDC-Kaiser ACE Study." Last modified April 2, 2019. cdc.gov/violenceprevention/childabuseandneglect/acestudy/about.html?CDC_AA_refVal=https%3A%2F%2Fwww.cdc.gov%2Fviolenceprevention%2Facestudy%2Fabout.html.

Chapman, Gary. *The Five Love Languages: The Secret to Love That Lasts.* Chicago: Northfield Publishing, 2015.

Coontz, Stephanie. *Marriage, A History.* New York: Penguin Books, 2014.

Fruzzetti, Alan E. *The High-Conflict Couple: Dialectical Behavior Therapy Guide to Finding Peace, Intimacy, and Validation.* San Francisco: New Harbinger Publications, 2006.

Gillespie, Brian Joseph, et al. "Close Adult Friendships, Gender, and the Life Cycle." *Journal of Social and Personal Relationships* 32, no. 6 (2015): 709–36. doi.org/10.1177/0265407514546977.

Gottman, John M. *The Marriage Clinic: A Scientifically Based Marital Therapy.* New York: W. W. Norton, 1999.

Gottman, John, and Nan Silver. *The Seven Principles for Making Marriage Work: A Practical Guide from the Country's Foremost Relationship Expert.* New York: Harmony, 1999.

Hardy, Janet W., and Dossie Easton. *The Ethical Slut: A Practical Guide to Polyamory, Open Relationships, and Other Freedoms in Sex and Love.* New York: Ten Speed Press, 2017.

Karen, Robert. *Becoming Attached: First Relationships and How They Shape Our Capacity to Love.* New York: Oxford University Press, 1998.

Levine, Amir, and Rachel S. F. Heller. *Attached: The New Science of Adult Attachment and How It Can Help You Find and Keep Love.* New York: TarcherPerigee, 2012.

Nagoski, Emily. *Come as You Are: The Surprising Science That Will Transform Your Sex Life.* New York: Simon and Schuster, 2015.

Patterson, Charlotte J., Erin L. Sutfin, and Megan Fulcher. "Division of Labor among Lesbian and Heterosexual Parenting Couples: Correlates of Specialized Versus Shared Patterns." *Journal of Adult Development* 11, no. 3 (2004): 179–89. doi.org/10.1023/B:JADE.0000035626.90331.47.

Pollitt, Amanda M., Brandon A. Robinson, and Debra Umberson. "Perceptions of Shared Power, Gender Conformity, and Marital Quality in Same- and Different-Sex Marriages." *PRC Research Brief Series* (2017). doi.org/10.1177/0891243217742110.

Swales, Michaela, Heidi L. Heard, and J. Mark G. Williams. "Linehan's Dialectical Behaviour Therapy (DBT) for Borderline Personality Disorder: Overview and Adaptation." *Journal of Mental Health* 9, no. 1 (2000): 7–23. doi.org/10.1080 /09638230016921.

UberKinky. "Periodic Table of Kink" (blog). *UberKinky*. November 10, 2014. uberkinky.co.uk/blog/periodic-table-of-kink.

Veaux, Franklin, and Eve Rickert. *More Than Two: A Practical Guide to Ethical Poly- amory*. Portland, OR: Thorntree Press, 2014.

Zosky, Diane L., and Robert Alberts. "What's in a Name? Exploring Use of the Word Queer as a Term of Identification within the College-Aged LGBT Commu- nity." *Journal of Human Behavior in the Social Environment*. 26, no. 7–8 (2016): 597–607. doi.org/10.1080/10911359.2016.1238803.

Zuzunaga, Andres. *Proposito*. 2011, https://www.cosmograma.com/proposito.php.

Index

Acknowledgments

A big thank-you to my friends and family for tolerating me as I completed my second book in one year. I miss you guys! Thank you for encouraging me to take care of myself, get out of the house, and have a little fun every once in a while.

Thank you to all my clients, who inspire me to write what I do, to become a better clinician, and to put all the energy I can into this truly weird field. I look forward to every session, and I am so grateful to you for being so vulnerable with me on a daily basis.

Thank you to Callisto Media for taking a chance on me and letting me pour my guts out yet again! It's been a blast.

About the Author

Emelie A. Blank, MA, LPC, is a therapist, supervisor candidate, speaker, podcaster, and writer. She graduated from Lewis & Clark College with a master of arts in Marriage, Couples, and Family Therapy, where her studies primarily focused on social justice and equity in the therapy practice as well as sex and relationship therapy. She works with individuals, families, and couples of all kinds out of the group practice that she owns and operates, Sprout Therapy PDX (sprouttherapypdx.com), in Portland, Oregon.

In her clinical work, Emelie most often works with the LGBTQIA+ community, folks exploring their sexuality, people experiencing burnout or vicarious trauma, people diagnosed with anxiety disorders, and folks struggling with "adulting." She uses an attachment lens in her work with supervisees and clients and has a soft spot for working with children of adoption, as she is one herself. She describes her therapy process as relatable, casual, and affirming, yet direct and effective.

Emelie also aims to provide access to free mental health education on her social media platforms. You can follow her on Instagram: @sprouttherapypdx.

She lives in Portland with her three cats, two dogs, and one human partner. She loves to spend time outdoors, traveling, and reading cheap thrillers.

If you enjoyed this title, check out Emelie's first book, *Easy Marriage Counseling: 52 Self-Guided Exercises to Deepen Your Relationship.*

CPSIA information can be obtained
at www.ICGtesting.com
Printed in the USA
BVHW051121160720
583793BV00002B/2